LIVING IN
TROUBLED
LANDS

Patrick Collins

LIVING IN
TROUBLED
LANDS

 *Beating the
Terrorist Threat
Overseas*

PALADIN PRESS
BOULDER, COLORADO

Living in Troubled Lands
by Patrick Collins

Copyright © 1981 by Patrick Collins

ISBN 0-87364-198-1
Printed in the United States of America

Published by Paladin Press, a division of
Paladin Enterprises, Inc.
Gunbarrel Tech Center
7077 Winchester Circle
Boulder, Colorado 80301 USA
+1.303.443.7250

Direct inquiries and/or orders to the above address.

PALADIN, PALADIN PRESS, and the "horse head" design
are trademarks belonging to Paladin Enterprises and
registered in United States Patent and Trademark Office.

Visit our Web site at www.paladin-press.com

For Dan, Brad, and Mat.

TABLE OF
CONTENTS

PART IV—APPENDIX

PREFACE

When my editors first advised me of their intent to rerelease this book, my initial instincts were that it would need to be updated. However, despite my additional years of experience and the worsening security conditions for Americans living abroad, a thorough review proved that there was little to change. The fundamentals of good personal security for the American abroad remain the same. So do the statistics, which clearly demonstrate that those who adhere to these fundamental security techniques significantly reduce their prospects for becoming victims of violence—no matter what the source.

In the ten years since this book's original publication, I have lived in Africa, Asia, the Middle East, and Latin America. Three of these locations presented serious threat levels: one for terrorist threats against Americans (where I was of known interest to the terrorist group), a second for an extremely high danger of violent criminal action, and a third for massive civil unrest and turmoil. I presently live in one of these locations where I have a high public profile and where, consequently, my personal security is at risk.

In essence, I have had to practice what I preach. It has not always been easy, it has not always been fun, and it has certainly not brought me to any point of blissful confidence whereby I feel I can rest on my expertise, stop worrying, and take my safety for granted. Unfortunately for Americans living abroad, personal security is a part-time job on a full-time basis. This change in life-style is the price one pays for the challenge, enjoyment, and benefit of living and working in most overseas locations.

If the last ten years of experience have not changed my views on the fundamentals of personal security, they have given me a perspective on a few points that are worth passing on:

- No matter where you live abroad, what you do, who you are, or what the actual threat level to your security, make sure that you are completely confident and satisfied with the security of your personal residence. Nothing will be more psychologically important to you and your family than the knowledge that your home abroad really is "your castle." This single factor will have more bearing on your enjoyment, outlook, and peace of mind than any other action you can take.

- The greatest threat to your personal security, regardless of where you live abroad or who presents the most danger to you, will come the moment you leave your residence and last until you are inside your business, office, club, compound, some shopping facilities, etc. It is imperative that you and your family understand that when you are inside these locations, you are basically on your turf; when you are outside them, you are on the bad guy's turf. While there are exceptions to this and every other rule, time has proven the fundamental veracity and universality of this one.

- The United States government does care about your well-being and safety abroad and devotes substantial resources in an effort to protect you and your fellow Americans. However, Uncle Sam is not your mother and is not going to send in the marines after you studiously ignored his advice. Your government's efforts are designed to help you help yourself. Listen to what the local U.S. embassy, consulate, or military officials have to say about local security conditions and what you should do to protect yourself. Register yourself with the consulate in order to be included on warning nets and evacuation plans. Read the pertinent Department of State Travel Advisories. And remember, the U.S. government doesn't like to show that it has been intimidated. If the embassy issues a warning order to U.S. citizens to leave the country, you can be certain that the situation is extremely serious.

- Lastly, one of the great benefits of being an American is that the Constitution protects your right to be stupid. When you are overseas, you will invariably meet fellow Americans who are exercising this cherished right by totally disregarding their own and their family's personal security. Close proximity to such blissful ignorance may cause you to doubt your own legitimate concerns and tempt you to forego the necessary change in life-style required to ensure your safety. Don't! There is usually a happy medium of good security to be found somewhere between total disregard and complete paranoia. In time, you will find it, and I guarantee that, in the long run, it will serve you well.

Having offered some advice from the perspective of the last ten years, it is appropriate to also look to the future. The world is changing and will never be the way it was before. Many countries are now committed to a level of economic interdependence that virtually guarantees that more and more Americans will move overseas to live and work. Democracy and pluralism are moving forward despite a rearguard action by old tyrants and new fanatics. Thus the threat of violence to Americans abroad will likely exist for some time to come. In essence, living overseas is no longer just an adventure, it's a job.

And that is just about the correct attitude to have regarding your personal security. It's no longer an option or an exciting aside to your new overseas assignment; it's just part of your job. Take it seriously, give it your best, and pay attention to details. Put in its proper perspective and given its necessary due, a good personal security plan will change your life-style a little and your odds of reaching old age a lot. Good luck.

—Patrick Collins
March 1991

INTRODUCTION

Living In Troubled Lands provides the American who must live, work, or travel overseas, with information that can substantially improve his or her own personal security. It lays to rest many widespread fallacies and misconceptions concerning the dangers facing Americans living abroad, and how the dangers can best be overcome.

Over the past few years the threat of violence has become an accepted part of life for many Americans living in Europe, South and Central America, and the Near and Far East. Little has been done to stop this violence and little can be done. With this in mind many Americans either have packed their bags and returned home or have resigned themselves to a life of "calculated risk." Certainly, a few Americans have had the luxury of expensive and sophisticated security systems, but they are a small minority. Help of a meaningful sort has simply not been available for the average person or family.

This state of affairs is due largely to the accepted notion that good personal security requires extensive professional training, or must be purchased at great expense. A corollary notion is that the only alternative to professional training or purchased security is to provide as many Americans as possible with some basic security tips . . . and wish them luck.

I believe that this line of thinking is erroneous. For most Americans, good personal security can be achieved without professional training and at minimum expense. What it requires is a strong knowledge of what personal security is and how it can be attained in the overseas environment, and a little time, effort, and determination on the part of the individual.

Put simply, my book provides overseas workers with an effective program by which they can:

1. Know and understand the threat they may face;
2. Analyze their own personal security situation;
3. Establish an effective personal security program;
4. Substantially reduce personal vulnerability to the violent threat;
5. Handle a threat that becomes a reality;
6. Survive a hostage or kidnap situation;
7. Enjoy a foreign tour of duty with a maximum amount of personal security at a minimum amount of cost and inconvenience.

Just how this book is used will vary from one individual to the next. Any security program must be designed to fit the individual's particular situation and needs. For example, the individual's identity, employer, lifestyle, and level and type of threat in the host country will all contribute to how this information is employed towards developing an effective personal security program.

Developing this program requires that the individual make logical and rational decisions regarding the suggestions I make. As the subtitle denotes, this book is a guide; not a specific set of directions. The reader must determine which advice is applicable to one's own situation, and how it can best be applied. All the elements of good personal security, regardless of the international location, are contained in this book. In order to effectively employ these techniques in your own situation you need only common sense, an interest in self-preservation, self-confidence, and a firm grasp of the fact that nobody cares as much about your personal security as you do.

PART I

REALITIES

"Personal security for the American abroad is a serious business. It cannot be taken for granted, nor can it be obtained through wishful thinking. It must be faced up to in a realistic manner. How well you perceive the realities of your own personal security situation will have a direct bearing on your very survival."

1
UNDERSTANDING THE PERSONAL SECURITY GAME

The next six chapters are devoted to answering the questions most commonly asked of me by Americans about to travel overseas to work and live. They are the same questions you would naturally ask a government expert, if you had the opportunity. After reading these chapters, it will be apparent that not all of the information pertains to every individual, as I mentioned before. However, all of the information is important in its own way; and even if you never need to use some of the more sophisticated advice, your understanding of this very critical problem will be considerably broadened. Such a broad knowledge will benefit your overall safety more than you may now realize.

What is personal security?
Personal security is the simple act of protecting yourself from physical harm. It is the accumulation of all the actions you have taken during your life to reduce or eliminate the chances of your being assaulted, attacked, beaten, molested, raped, or murdered. In fact, you practice personal security to varying degrees every day of your life. You have locks on your doors, you avoid high crime areas, you are careful of strangers, and you may even keep a gun at home. All of these are basic and elementary techniques of personal security. To a large degree, you take these steps in order to protect yourself and your family from the threat of violence. And the length to which you go in

in order to protect yourself and your family is largely dependent upon how serious you deem the threat.

Because you are an American and have probably lived in the United States for the major part of your life, you are familiar with the potential dangers that exist there, and you have a basic understanding about how to protect yourself from them. But what about overseas? What about the dangers to your personal security there? You may be a stranger in a strange land. The people, the customs, the land, and the language may all be inscrutably different. Will you be able to protect yourself? Will you be able to take the same responsible precautions there that you have taken while living in the United States? And will they be enough?

That is what this book is all about. It is designed to help you achieve a level of security and a feeling of confidence much like you had in the United States. And in particular it will help you deal with those special dangers that exist for Americans living abroad today: terrorism and violence, in all their forms.

What is a personal security program?

A personal security program is the thoughtful, realistic, and religiously practiced method by which you attempt to protect yourself from harm. It is the accumulation of all the actions you take, all the defenses you build, and all the methods you employ in order to maintain your personal security. Above all it is a program of positive action with definite requirements, standards, and goals. You will need to develop a personal security program of your own which will integrate all your plans, actions, and requirements into a cohesive format that will serve as both a guide and measuring stick toward achieving a high degree of personal security. Your ultimate objective should be to develop a program which fully serves your needs and provides for a maximum amount of security with a minimum amount of expense or inconvenience.

Do I need a personal security program?

Everyone needs a personal security program. The depth of that program and its level of sophistication is determined by your particular situation and needs. As an American living in another country the chances are you will need a plan which is substantially more complete and in depth than one you might use while in the United States.

Since I am not a security specialist, shouldn't I get some professional help?

You should get all the professional help you can as long as it doesn't cost *you* money. Whether you work for government or industry you should try to get your organization to provide you with all the security assistance it can offer. But don't put blind faith in any type of outside help you receive.

There are no pat answers or solutions in the field of personal security. What works for you may not work for the next person. There are also very few real experts and they are difficult to discern from the self-proclaimed experts. So getting reliable help may be a challenge.

What is important to realize is that good personal security depends largely on knowledge, common sense, and decision-making. If you take personal security seriously and are willing to work at it, the chances are that you can do a good job on your own. You may not have any other choice.

If it's dangerous overseas, maybe I shouldn't go?

If your only concern is the danger, you probably *should* go. There are very few places in the world where the danger to you will be such that it would be in your best interest to stay home. The chances are that with a little care and planning you will be able to live a safe and enjoyable life at your new destination.

How can I enjoy my overseas tour if I have to worry about personal security?

By developing a good personal security plan and having complete confidence that it will work. And if you have a good plan it *will* work.

2
THE AMERICAN ABROAD

Who lives abroad and why?

Today, over 1.5 million Americans live outside of the United States and its territories. They are government employees, military personnel, businessmen and women, diplomats, students, professionals, clergy, retirees, and a myriad of other groups, who by choice or obligation must live and work overseas. Their reasons for being overseas are as varied as their occupations. Some choose to go simply to see a foreign land, others to enhance their career opportunities, and still others to help the country's native people. But for most Americans, living overseas is an obligation connected with their employment. Be it military or government service, business requirements or simply the advantages of better pay with the hope of a better future, most Americans live overseas because the business of making a living demands it.

Why worry about personal security?

All Americans overseas should be concerned with their personal security. This is because of political and social turbulence, and a consistently high rate of violence directed at Americans in many locations throughout the world today. The simple fact that an individual is an American citizen may make him an ideal target for a number of violent gangs overseas, be they criminal or terrorist. In many areas of the world violence is the primary means by which radical groups hope to effect political change. These groups often equate the individual American citizen with the United States government and its

7

domestic and foreign policies. It happens that they may feel an attack upon the American government may be beneficial in achieving their political or social goals at home. By the process of proxy, the American in that foreign land may be viewed by these elements as representative of the American government, and thus represents a viable political target of violence.

As an American you are also stuck with another national image: that of being rich. While this may seem a bit preposterous in today's world of inflation and the declining dollar, images die hard and this one is no exception. In many parts of the world Americans are still considered to be the richest and the most affluent of all the "foreigners." It should also be remembered that in a number of areas, especially third world countries, Americans are in fact rich by local standards. More importantly, the companies for whom individual Americans work are often viewed in a like manner, and are assumed to be both willing and able to pay ransom and extortion money for their employees.

Real or imagined, both the radical and terrorist elements and the common criminal may find the average American a worthy target of their violence, if only from a monetary point of view. Even though you're only an "average everyday American working abroad" you may be of considerable interest to the practitioners of violence in your new home.

Who are these violent elements?

Insofar as this book is concerned, these violent elements are any group, organization, or individual in a foreign country that may present a threat to your personal security and/or the personal security of your family. They include political terrorists, criminal terrorists, urban guerrillas, revolutionary groups, "liberation" groups, radical militant elements of both the left and right, street demonstrators and mobs, and common criminals. All of these groups will be discussed in more detail in later chapters. It is only important at this point to note the large variety of violent groups which may pose a threat to you overseas.

How dangerous is living abroad?

In most cases living abroad poses no special danger, assuming you have a basic personal security plan, are reasonably careful, and do not have a high-threat profile in a known high-threat area. Generally, only those persons who live in an extremely active terrorist environment, and are high level executives with high public profiles, need be greatly concerned. This type of individual is a high probability target and must conduct his security in a manner reflecting understanding that he is a likely target of an extortion, kidnapping or assassination plan. Fortunately, only a very few Americans need worry about this problem, and they are well aware of who they are.

How does the average American working overseas handle the threat of violence now?

Unfortunately, the answer to this question is short and clear: he doesn't. Other than for certain groups of governmental and military personnel assigned overseas, there has been little effort to help the individual American cope with the problem of personal security abroad. This lack of assistance is not, however, due to benign neglect on the part of the United States government or private industry. Rather, it is the result of a general lack of useful information on the subject and an inability to determine what type of assistance would be both meaningful and cost-effective. There are also considerable economic and political obstacles involved with trying to help so many people, in so many different places, with such a wide variety of problems. These obstacles are generally perceived as being insurmountable.

Of the various attempts that have been made to help the average American abroad, *none has proved effective for widespread application.* Some United States corporations have instituted training programs in personal security for their senior and mid-level personnel being assigned to another country. The government has attempted to disseminate basic information on personal security for the executive abroad. A few private security firms have offered personal security training programs to the U.S. business community and industry. The quality of these programs is sometimes good, but in point of fact, only a very small number of Americans have been able to undergo this type of training due to the expense involved and the necessary allocation of time off from work.

The only other effort to help the individual American with this problem has come in the form of books and manuals. Unfortunately these works have generally taken an academic point of view, have been directed only at the very high level executive living abroad, or have not been made available for sale to the general public. I should also mention that such manuals usually cost over $100!

So, as we can see, previous attempts to help the average American working overseas have been less than adequate.

How successful have Americans been at beating the threat of violence?

At present, no clearinghouse for these statistics exists. Some general observations can be made, though. To me, most Americans involved in kidnap or assassination threats represent the statistics of our own failure to adequately protect ourselves and ensure our personal security. In fact, most American victims received little or no personal security training and took few, if any, precautions on their own behalf to prevent such incidents. A few of these victims were provided with sophisticated security systems or protection. In most of these cases, they or their security staff flagrantly violated at least one of the basic rules of good personal security. This failure led directly to the success of the effort against them. On the other hand, there are cases of persons who were adequately trained, had good security systems and practices, and who still became victims of kidnapping or violent assault. Even the best of efforts will not always beat a determined foe who has chosen you as his victim.

On the brighter side, there are cases of persons who have defeated or thwarted their would-be attackers. Sometimes this was the result of good security practices, sometimes by the simple use of common sense at the appropriate time, and sometimes by luck. The substantial portion of those who succeeded have attributed their success to a solid understanding of good personal security and religious adherence to a good personal security program.

Of ultimate importance is the fact that good personal security practices lead not so much to patently defeating the violent threat against the targetted individual, but rather to keeping the individual from becoming a target in the first place. This is the basic keynote in good personal security for the American abroad, and is the single most important aspect over which you, the individual, have considerable control.

3
KNOWING
YOUR ENEMY

Why is knowing your enemy so important?

Knowing your enemy is important because it will directly influence the degree of security you will need, and the manner in which your personal security program must be employed. In the ultimate sense, your knowledge of the enemy will have a direct bearing on your very survival. Knowing your enemy helps you to prepare your defenses. It provides you with the information needed to take adequate and reasonable steps to defend yourself against the enemy's potential threat. It is an integral part of what you must learn and understand if you are to remain safe in the threat environment.

How will knowing my enemy affect my personal security plan?

This knowledge will give you a set of parameters to guide you in developing your own personal security plan. If your enemy is weak, few in number, and ineffective, your personal security plan will not have to be so sophisticated as it might necessarily be if the enemy is strong, numerous, and extremely capable. A knowledge of your enemy's methods, goals, and capabilities will in the same manner assist you in developing specific defenses. Understanding who has been targetted as victims, and why, will give you the added ability of knowing if you are actually a potential target victim and if so, how you might remove yourself from this category. Generally speaking, a good overall knowledge and understanding of your enemy will provide the means by which you can prepare your personal security defenses in a manner that is both realistic and effective.

Generally speaking, who is my enemy?

Your enemy is anyone in your overseas location who would willfully pick you as a target for kidnapping, murder, assassination, bombing, extortion, assault, or any other form of violence or terror. Naturally, this list cannot include any of the above which are crimes of passion, or crimes that are the result of criminal behavior on your part.

Who are the specific groups that present a danger to me abroad?

The specific groups which may pose a threat to you individually are too numerous to name here and change too quickly for me to provide a comprehensive description for each of them. You must be the one to gather information on the groups that may affect you, and you can do so by employing the methods discussed in chapter 5. For now, let's discuss the major types of groups, what they are, how they operate, and how they may affect you.

TERRORISTS

Unfortunately, the word terrorist has been loosely used by the media and has come to represent any group, element, or individual who uses violent action to achieve a political goal. If this were actually the case, most armies—and all revolutionary armies, including George Washington's—would have to be called terrorists. It seems the definition of *terrorist* now totally depends on who commits the violent action, and who does the subsequent name-calling. For our purposes, a terrorist is defined as an individual who commits actions which are politically or socially motivated, and which would be deemed by most Americans to be unjust, immoral, indiscriminate, and outrageous.

Terrorist groups are generally composed of a small number of persons who achieve notoriety for their causes disproportionate to the size of their actual following, disproportionate even to the real impact of the violent deeds they perform to achieve notoriety. The Japanese Red Army of Japan, Black September of the Middle East, and the Red Army Faction of Europe are just a few of those groups which can definitely be called terrorists. These groups undertake violent actions which often appear to have no moral bounds and little rational direction. They are the most violent in their approach, the most indiscriminate in their choice of victims, and the most dangerous in terms of your personal security. If any of these types of groups operate in your overseas location and target Americans, you will have to take extra care in the preparation of your security plan. While the chances of becoming a target of one of these groups is extremely small, only an excellent personal security program will deter these groups from success should you become a target.

These groups operate in a fairly consistent manner. They use only the most violent methods to accomplish their goals: kidnapping, assassination, bombing, robbery, hostage-taking and similar activities. Their victims generally fall into two categories: highly selected individuals who serve as political targets, and innocent people whose victimization will illustrate the terrorists' capacity for terror, and therefore help them achieve political goals. The terrorists' operational goal is often to instill terror in the local population and a lack of confidence in the local government. In this regard, their methods are often effective.

There are two other aspects of the known terrorist groups that have come to light lately and are worth discussing. One is the emergence of an international terrorist front, and the other is terrorism simply for the sake of terrorism. The international terrorist front has been manifested by the growing number of joint operations involving two or more terrorist groups who supposedly have different motivations and goals. This is illustrated by the joint operations of Black September and the Japanese Red Army, and the Red Army Faction of West Germany and the Red Brigade of Italy. This method of one terrorist group assisting another has presented a new problem for government and business, and made it more difficult to defend against terrorist actions.

Terrorism simply for the sake of terrorism has added a new dimension to the whole role of the terrorist. No matter how distorted, it makes the practice of terrorism itself an industry rather than a means to a political end. It also makes terrorism a capitalist venture, since terrorism practiced in this manner is usually designed to make the terrorist wealthy rather than to achieve pure political goals. Just how these new aspects of terrorism affect you, the individual American, is that the use of joint operations by terrorists reduces your ability to clearly identify your enemy; and the use of terrorism simply for financial gain makes you a more promising target, especially in terms of kidnapping for ransom.

The importance of *knowing* the true terrorist who may operate in your foreign location cannot be overstressed. While this type may be the least active, the least numerous, and the least visible, it is also the least constrained by ordinary moral standards. Therefore, true terrorists are the most dangerous of all your potential enemies.

CRIMINAL TERRORISTS

Criminal terrorists present a special threat to the American living abroad. Their objective is almost always financial gain. They copy the terrorists' methods in order to make money. Their primary means of accomplishing this goal is through kidnapping, threats, and extortion. They use the terrorists' methods for three reasons. First, these methods are often the most effective means of criminally obtaining large sums of cash. Second, the operational techniques employed by the terrorist offer the criminal a minimum amount of risk and a maximum potential for profit. Third, the criminal act itself may be sufficiently disguised to make both the victim and the local authorities believe that a true terrorist element is involved, covering the criminal's tracks.

Unfortunately for the individual American, criminal terrorists are often not as intelligent and informed as real terrorists are. So the criminal terrorist is not as realistic about choosing targets and obtaining money. The result is that many of these criminal terrorists fall into that category of people who believe that most Americans are rich and able to make ransom or extortion payoffs, thus including a larger group of people within their category of prey. However, there can be a beneficial side to this. The criminal terrorist is generally interested only in money. It is unlikely that political demands made by criminal terrorist kidnappers will actually have to be met in order to obtain the release of one of their victims. In these cases, negotiators, working on the release of the victim, can concentrate on the more simplistic issue of money and the more complex problem of ensuring that the victim will be returned—alive.

If you are certain that criminal terrorists are targetting Americans in your area, here is one simple precautionary measure to take. Keep a low profile. This may sound obvious but please think about it. If the criminal terrorists do not know you are an American living in their area of operation, they certainly cannot pick you as a target.

URBAN GUERRILLA AND REVOLUTIONARY GROUPS

Urban guerrilla and revolutionary groups are militant factions seeking economic, social, or political change. These groups normally have the support of some segment of the local population. Typically, urban guerrillas and revolutionaries operate in one particular country, seek the support of the local population, and generally create definite goals. They believe these goals are just and moral, and in the best interest of the entire population.

Such groups range from very small ultra-leftist student groups, to full-fledged guerrilla armies controlling major geographic areas of the host country. Usually, these groups are comprised of local residents. What motivates them is a zealous belief in the justness of their cause. Furthermore, they are convinced that armed struggle is the only way their goals can be attained. While many of these groups do practice various degrees of terrorist activity, their need to gain the support of the local citizenry generally inhibits indiscriminate terrorism. They also tend to show a greater degree of humanity than the strictly terrorist organization. Ultimately, what separates these groups from the strictly terrorist elements is their need for the support of the local population, and their belief that this is more effectively obtained through propaganda and direct armed confrontation with the local government, rather than by terrorizing large segments of the local population.

How these groups will affect you is entirely dependent upon the particular makeup, methods, and goals of the terrorist elements you will face in your particular overseas location. The mere fact that these groups exist and are operating in your location does not necessarily mean they pose a definite threat to you. While most of these groups do consider some types of Americans as potential targets, this is not always the case. The Irish Republican Army has never been considered a serious threat to Americans living in its areas of operations. Nicaragua's Sandanistas did not target against American citizens. Other groups avoid targetting Americans for tactical reasons. Clearly, it is important to analyze each urban/revolutionary group on an individual basis.

Many of these groups do, however, target Americans simply because they are *Americans*. They see us as the representatives of a system and ideology opposed to their own. Targetting Americans can also embarrass the local government and indirectly attack the United States government. Others do so simply because Americans seem likely targets for obtaining money through kidnapping and extortion, so the group can further finance its cause. Lastly, some urban guerrilla and revolutionary groups hold the credo that you are either with them or against them. Here you will always be a potential target as long as you live in their area of operations.

Urban guerrillas and revolutionary groups tend to use similar methods, and are often elements of the same political movement. Their home territories may be somewhat different, though. Urban guerrillas operate in urban areas and cities. They generally live in secret, and only clandestinely engage in armed operations. Their tactics often are similar to terrorist actions, which the urban guerrillas generally direct at the host government and its high profile supporters rather than against innocent persons. Guerrillas spend a lot of time recruiting members for their organization, distributing propaganda, performing intelligence missions, and planning and committing terrorist-style acts. Bombings, kidnappings, woundings, and occasionally assassinations are the terrorist actions preferred by urban guerrillas. If they are part of a larger revolutionary group, they may well coordinate their actions with those of sympathetic comrades in the field.

The true revolutionary group, on the other hand, often has firm control over an entire territory, and will even declare a revolutionary government in this territory. At miminum a group consists of a few active members who operate openly as soldiers in the field. They may use hit-and-run tactics, or directly engage in combat with elements of the local government's army. In most instances they will also have clandestine urban guerrilla forces in the cities. Both openly and through clandestine means, the revolutionary group challenges the authority and legitimacy of the local government.

When operating in the field, revolutionaries undertake operations ranging from hit-and-run guerrilla actions to operations similar to conventional military tactics. They will also use terrorist tactics when deemed appropriate, but by the nature of the situation these are generally limited to full-scale attacks, asssassinations, or kidnappings. The great danger of these groups is that they are seldom shown mercy by the host government and its army. They likewise show no mercy toward anyone considered an enemy.

Urban guerrilla and revolutionary groups operate on virtually every continent, ranging from groups that are small and poorly organized, to a few with tons of the latest military equipment—and plenty of men to use it.

LIBERATION GROUPS

A true liberation group seeks to depose the government of their native country through armed intervention, on the grounds that it is illegitimate or does not represent "the people." Classic examples of liberation groups are ZANU and ZAPU of the Zimbabwe-Rhodesian Patriotic Front, and the Southwest Africa's People's Organization (SWAPO) attempting to take control of Namibia from the South Africans. Liberation groups normally take the form of regular military units, often based outside the target country. Their troops are natives of the country they try to overthrow. The efforts of these regular units are augmented by clandestine organizations within the target country, which provide intelligence and terrorist-style support. The primary mode of operation for liberation groups is guerrilla warfare, combined with terrorist actions and regular combat unit engagement with the target country's armed forces. Liberation groups affect the security of Americans just as urban guerrillas and revolutionaries do.

MILITANT RADICALS

Militant radical groups take many forms, and plague nearly every country in the world. They may be ideologically to the left or right, fanatically religious, extremely nationalistic, or of a dozen other persuasions. What brings them all under this category is the fact that they believe in their causes so strongly that they tend to resort to violence as either a means to force their beliefs upon others, or simply to vent their rage on opponents. What differentiates them from the rest of these groups is that their hostile actions are often not as severe or numerous as the other groups, and are generally not well-planned. The radicals involved may even act openly and neither attempt to hide their identities nor avoid capture by the police.

Most of these radical militants frequent the campuses of universities or social circles made up of intellectuals and artists. They are generally young, idealistic, and frustrated because the rest of the world doesn't see things the way they do. They are often the sons and daughters of the middle and upper classes. What makes them a danger is not so much what violent actions they take, but what these actions can lead to. Worst of all, they are often the pawns of one of the more deadly threat groups.

Hostile actions taken by these groups often take aim at American citizens and institutions abroad. The demonstration that turns into a full-scale riot and the subsequent firebombings of American cars and residences are typical results of the radical militants' actions. In terms of planning personal security, militant radicals certainly deserve your attention. Yet it is more important to determine what their actions may lead to, rather than simply what they are.

THREAT GOVERNMENTS

A threat government is any government inclined to take hostile action against you without legal due process or just cause. It is also any government which, intentionally or unintentionally, does not control any of its subordinate entities (police, army, etc.) that threaten your personal security. A most recent example of a threat government is provided by Iran, ruled by the Ayatollah Khomeini. In essence the fifty-two American hostages held there by student militants are ultimately the victims of Iran's irrational leader. In Iran and similar nations, you are just as likely to be victimized by the state's soldiers, as you are by common criminals. Or right wing elements might assassinate you and then blame it on the left wing, or vice versa.

From this you can see that a threat government is probably more dangerous than any other hostile group. It is easy to be lulled into a false sense of security in these threat nations. Their hostile actions and operational techniques are limited only by the imagination.

Fortunately, accurate information on most threat governments is easily obtained. As Iran showed us, a hasty evacuation may be called for, if the government's threat to your own security becomes apparent.

MOBS AND DEMONSTRATORS

Mobs are groups of emotionally-charged people who commit mass acts of violence that are relatively spontaneous, though pre-planned mob actions do occur. Essentially what we are examining is the threat posed to you by a riot or mob action. This is important to consider when one examines the civil unrest prevalent in so many parts of the world today. Mob action can take many forms and most of you are familiar with them. Rock throwing, firebombing, burning, assault, theft, destruction and murder are all common forms of mob-related violence. Mob action often winds up being directed at the local American population, usually as a result of guided incitement by a few leaders whose actions are more planned than spontaneous.

Intelligence information on these leaders may make it possible to predict the mob actions they plan. But since this prior knowledge is hard to come by, it is generally difficult to predict riots in advance. And many riots are *not* preplanned anyway. Even more difficult is discerning whether or not the mob action may affect your security and, if so, in what manner. The anti-mob defensive techniques I present later are based on the possibility that mob action *may* occur in your location, that the specific types of action occurring may range from the mild to the severe, and that you may be the target of such action.

COMMON CRIMINALS

While it may seem strange to include the common criminal in a book that discusses terrorists, it is in fact quite logical. There is little point in defending yourself against all the previously discussed groups, only to leave yourself open to assault by a common criminal. Additionally, the vast majority of you will probably never be exposed to the more violent groups. But you may very well encounter the criminal element responsible for much of the violence and death in the world today. Therefore, defending yourself against the common criminal should be an integral part of your personal security plan.

Most of you are well aware of the common criminal's methods and targets. In this respect the common criminal in the United States is little different from the one you will meet overseas. But there are some variations and these should be noted. First, in some parts of the world crime is more artful and the ingenuity of the perpetrators more formidable. Second, in many parts of the world crime is not a means of getting ahead but is rather a means of survival; thus the criminal is more determined and will take greater risks. Third, in some non-western countries the value of life is not held in such high esteem as it is in this country. The taking of life is accomplished with greater ease and less hesitation. When you combine these three points with the commonly accepted notion overseas that all Americans are rich, it is easy to understand why the common criminal and violent crime are dangers which you should take seriously.

**Since many of these groups appear similar,
how will I know which one is which?**

Many of these groups *are* similar, and in fact will often fit into several of the previously described categories at the same time. My primary reason for breaking these groups down is to give you some understanding of the differences that can and do occur in the makeup and actions of the various types of hostile organizations. The fact that a person is a militant does not necessarily make him a revolutionary, and the fact that one is a revolutionary does not necessarily mean he is also a terrorist. Each group cannot be considered solely by its name or category, but must be known for what hostile actions it undertakes, who its potential targets are, and how that may directly affect your own security.

You don't judge a book by its cover so don't judge the violent elements in your area by their "trade" name. Determine if they are *your* enemy and if so, learn all you can about them.

4
TAKING CHARGE,
TAKING ACTION

Who's in charge?

You are! It is *your* life, *your* family, and *your* personal security program. No one can do a better job of it than you can if you put your mind to it. This does not mean that you should avoid seeking all the advice and assistance you can. It does mean, though, that you must be the one who makes the final decisions, based upon any help and assistance you have received. If you are going it alone and realize that you are not going to get much help, then this makes the decision pretty simple: you must take charge because there is no alternative.

However, you may be one of the lucky few who will have some professional help, maybe a corporate security officer or personal guards. If this is the case, then take the help, but take heed! Just because you have some help does not mean you can forget about your own security. While these people may try their very best to protect you, they can make mistakes. You must be able to detect these mistakes and take the proper corrective action. For instance, when you get in a cab, do not let the driver go 100 miles per hour just because he has a chauffer's license. Tell him to slow down because you know it's dangerous. The reason you know it's dangerous is because you know how to drive yourself and you have common sense.

In like fashion, you must learn everything you can about personal security and use your common sense when called for. You must make the decisions by giving tacit approval when you know your security help is right and by making forceful decisions when they are wrong. Thus, every individual must be his own chief of security and his own decision maker, regardless of the circumstances.

Now that I'm in charge, what is my first course of action?

By simply picking up this book and reading this far you have begun the first necessary course of action: that is, to gain knowledge. But, while this book attempts to cover all the necessary facets of personal security for the American abroad, reading it is by no means all that you need do. You should continue to read and learn as much about personal security as you can. In addition, you should make a serious effort to learn everything you can about the country in which you will live, its history, customs, culture, social and political problems, and its people. In the game of personal security, knowledge is your first line of defense.

What is my second course of action?

Your second course of action is to plan and prepare. This will be accomplished by developing your personal security program. Your program development should take place as you read this book. Carefully read each chapter noting the guidelines, explanations, and recommendations. Judge how the information affects you personally and note actions you should take which are appropriate to your particular situation and needs. When you have finished reading this book, examine your notes and compare them with the comprehensive checklists in Part IV. This done, sit down with your husband or wife (who should also read this book) and work out a detailed personal security program. Mental preparedness cannot be overemphasized. Think about what you will do in the crunch!

What is my third course of action?

Your third course of action is to put your knowledge and program to use. Your program will serve no purpose unless practiced daily until it becomes an integral part of your lifestyle. By following your personal security program and continuing to gain knowledge you will be able to make further refinements in your defenses and make changes as the situation demands. This is the only way that good personal security can be achieved and maintained.

Are there any other actions I should take?

Just one. Make the most out of your foreign tour by relaxing, enjoying yourself and doing all those exciting things you have planned. Unless you are in an unusually dangerous situation, you will have little need to worry so long as you have a good security program and follow it faithfully. In very few cases will this mean battening down the hatches and living the life of a recluse. Do whatever you want to do so long as it does not violate your security plan or put you in danger. Make the most out of what might be a real adventure and one of the fondest memories of your life. In essence, pay attention to security but do not become paranoid about it.

5
THE INFORMATION PROGRAM

Why will I need more information than is found in this book?

Simply because *knowledge is your first line of defense,* and because this book cannot answer all of the questions you will have regarding your own location and problems. A generalized book cannot specifically answer such questions as *where* is the safest part of town to live, *what* terrorist groups operate in your overseas location, or *who* has the best security guards for rent. Thus, there will be questions you will have to find answers to yourself—unless you can afford a security consultant.

How will I know what information I need?

In most cases this will be obvious. For other cases, I have noted specific types of information needed to develop security programs and to gain a solid understanding of the local security situation.

Where will I find the information I need?

Most of the necessary information can be obtained through the offices of the United States government, from private industry (including your own company), from the local government, from the media and other publications, and from overseas and American friends.

What type of information can each of these groups give me?

U.S. GOVERNMENT

Your own government can provide you with a considerable amount of information relating to your host country, the local security situation, and how Americans fare in the local environment. This type of information is obtainable from the Department of State, the Department of Commerce, and the United States embassy located in your host country. Much of this information is available free in pamphlet form. Furthermore, specific questions of a more personal nature can usually be answered by the embassy security officer or embassy political officer. They are there to help you and in most cases will do their best to do so. The embassy is also a good source of information on the local laws and how they might affect your security planning. The following is extracted verbatim from Department of State Publication 8884, Department and Foreign Service Series 157 (January 1977):

"American embassies and consulates will advise any American citizen or business representative who requests information on possible terrorist threats in foreign countries. The security officer or other designated officer at a diplomatic or consular post can provide the following information:

the nature, if any, of the general terrorist threat in a particular country;

whether private American citizens or companies have been the target of terrorist threats or attacks, in the recent past;

specific areas of the cities or countryside that are considered dangerous for foreigners;

recommended host government contacts including police officials;

local employment requirements for private security services;

methods and agencies available for security and background checks on local employees;

local laws and regulations concerning ownership, possession, and registration of weapons;

U.S. government policy on ransom and blackmail;

steps to take in case of a terrorist threat or act.

In the case of a terrorist action against an American citizen or company, the Embassy or consulate can:

facilitate communication with the home office and the family of the victim if normal channels are not adequate;

help establish useful liaison with local authorities;

provide information and suggest possible alternatives open to the family of the victim or his company. The U.S. government, however, cannot decide whether or not to accede to terrorist demands. Such a decision can be made only by the family or company of the victim, but it should be in consonance with local law. (U.S. policy, as publicly stated, is not to make any concessions to terrorists demands.)"

If the embassy is far away from your location within the host country, you should consider contacting the nearest consulate. The consul general and his staff are also kept posted on changing political and security conditions within the country and can usually provide you with the same help as the embassy. A visit to the consulate is also important in order for you to register yourself and your family with them. This is necessary for a variety of reasons but primarily because it includes your name on any emergency evacuation plan, which is no small point if the local situation really starts to turn sour.

In addition to obtaining information from the government, you should carefully consider any information they volunteer. If at any time they advise you that the local situation is deteriorating or could become dangerous—believe it. The government is not always right, but the odds are they know a lot more about it than you do. If you are ever advised, officially or unofficially, by any member of the American embassy, attaches office, or consular corps, that a threat exists on your life— leave the country immediately. The government does not casually make statements of this kind. They are often the result of information provided by good sources which cannot be disclosed. Unfortunately, more than one American in recent years has disregarded this type of warning and paid for it with his life. So heed what American officials in the host country are saying. They get paid to know what is going on and most of them do a good job of it. If for any reason you do not agree with their estimation of a security situation, make sure your view is the more critical one. To do otherwise may be taking an unnecessary risk.

AMERICAN PRIVATE INDUSTRY

American private industry abroad can also be a good source of information on a variety of security-related topics. Many companies have extensive experience overseas and some have security officers assigned to their overseas offices. Your own company may fit this category. These are excellent sources of information on such things as how to obtain reliable and trustworthy domestic help, what guard services to use, the most secure place to live, etcetera. So start with your own company. If it cannot help, contact other American companies in your location. Most will be more than happy to help you all they can.

You might also consider contacting, and joining, your local chapter of the host country American Chamber of Commerce. This is not only an excellent way of obtaining useful information but also of introducing yourself to the local business community.

The American private security industry is international and many of the firms offering burglar alarms, security systems, or guard services have offices overseas. These firms are worth contacting should you need information on security hardware. They are usually reliable when it comes to hardware but should be given a thorough examination when discussing questions relating to guard services or other personnel-related security problems. Remember, they are in business to sell products or services, so some of their advice may be prejudiced to their advantage.

HOST COUNTRY GOVERNMENTS

These, along with their subordinate organizations such as state governments and local police, can also be used as a source of information on numerous security-related topics. While you will generally find them more than willing to be of assistance, you should be cautious about the validity of their information. Most host governmental organizations feel obliged to provide only rosy pictures of the local security situation and will go to great lengths to convince the foreign business community that the country is both stable and secure. This is especially true in third world countries which are highly dependent upon the other nations to keep their economies going. It is not so true in certain Western countries where dangerous conditions are generally considered temporary and controllable. Ordinarily, one of your best sources of information on existing threat groups, their level of activity, the criminal element, and basic security practices relative to the local situation will be the local police department. In most cases you should seek the advice of a high ranking police official rather than the officer pounding the beat. However, make sure he is a professional police officer rather than a political appointee. And be careful, since many such police are corrupt, yet may appear to be honest.

Rather than simply seeking occasional advice from your local police contact, you should attempt to develop a relationship with him (if you trust him *completely*), ensuring both reliable and timely advice from him regarding changing security conditions. This is best done by including the officer as one of your group of foreign friends. Invite him to your parties, have him meet your family, and take him out to lunch occasionally. In this manner you can develop a relationship which is based upon friendship rather than business. As a friend he will be much more likely to look out for your welfare, with his subordinates paying particular attention to your security. He will also be more inclined to give you an accurate picture of the security problems that truly exist, rather than a programmed recital of approved government propaganda.

If you are unable to establish a friendship with your local police official, or just do not trust him, then attempt to make friends with a member of the local government who is in a position to know what the real security situation is. While he may not be as good a source as the police officer, he could prove to be a valuable asset to your program.

A few more words of caution are in order. Never discuss your own personal security program with any foreign official. Never attempt to establish a friendship with any government or police official who you may feel could be a member of a threat organization. Never associate with any government or police official who is a known target of any threat group. Your simple association with him will raise your profile and may make you a target yourself.

LOCAL INFORMATION MEDIA

Newspapers, magazines, radio, and TV are good sources of general information on the political, economic, social, and security conditions that exist in your host country. Reading a variety of the printed publications (I suggest learning the local language) will help give you another valuable perspective on the situation in the country and what the future may hold. This may appear to be an obvious point, but many Americans living overseas have absolutely no idea about what is happening in their host country. So read everything you can. If you have a problem with the foreign language, try to find local English language publications. A short-wave radio receiver capable of picking up Voice of America or BBC broadcasts is indispensable for both the home and office. Listen to English language broadcasts if they are available. If necessary, have a friend who speaks the local language read the paper to you or at least give you highlights of the local news.

While the information media are a good source of general information they must also be judged by their quality and the conditions under which they operate. If there is censorship you must attempt to judge how much this distorts accuracy and just how much and what type of information is being censored. If the press and other media are under complete government control, then you must assume that much of what you hear and read may be inaccurate. Also, the media can be guilty of overstatements, distortions, and fabrications. So be realistic. Look for general information that is corroborated by a variety of sources.

FOREIGN AND AMERICAN FRIENDS AND ASSOCIATES

This group can, at the same time, be your best and worst sources of information. They can provide you with both important and useful information, as well as absolute trash. Which type of information you get will depend largely upon the individual providing the information. There are no hard and fast rules about judging the quality of the information you are receiving. Rather, you must judge the source. Look for someone whom you respect, who is honest, and who will say "I don't know" when he does not know. Look for someone who is also concerned about security in the same way you are, but who has an extensive amount of experience in the host country. Above all, seek a friend or associate who is logical, rational, and realistic. He will not be so prone to the two extremes of paranoia and overconfidence when discussing security-related problems. Once again, do not trust *anyone* with the details of your own personal security plan. That knowledge must remain with you and your family and perhaps one other trusted friend or colleague, preferably an American.

The types of information you might seek from your friends and colleagues cover a broad spectrum but should be limited to information which they might reasonably be expected to answer with some degree of personal knowledge and experience. This would include questions relating to safe areas to live, persons or areas to avoid, reliable locksmiths and burglar alarm firms, the reliability of local police, specific problems regarding local crime, safe schools for your children, and so forth. These are important questions you will have upon arriving at your foreign destination which deserve the most accurate answers you can find.

Will any information be provided me automatically?
The only information you will almost certainly receive without asking for it will be provided by the local "rumor mill." Most of you are acquainted with rumor mills as they exist in most every neighborhood, club, and business in the United States. Likewise, be prepared to hear much erroneous information overseas. The rumor mills that abound in the American communities abroad would make the Soviet KGB's Disinformation Section proud. Never have so few contributed to misinforming so many, so often, and so completely. These rumor mills are a tribute to the American imagination and our nation-

al ability to take elements of the dull truth and turn them into breathtaking fiction.

Despite their innocent nature, these rumor mills can play a large role in undermining your security. While they generally deal in the mundane gossip of their own little Peyton Place, they often go into high gear when the local security situation begins to deteriorate or at least appears to deteriorate. The result is that as tensions increase, an abundance of erroneous information is promulgated for anyone who will listen. Almost without exception this information will present a distorted picture of the situation: one which is either vastly exaggerated or completely glossed over. Were you to use the rumor mill as a source of information during a time of crisis or instability you would almost certainly be misinformed.

The point is: make sure that when security problems occur in your location that you turn to reliable sources for your information. Rumors and rumor mills make for good gossip on the cocktail circuit but have no place whatsoever in your security planning or information gathering, whether it is in a time of crisis or total calm. If what you hear is interesting if true, then verify or negate it by checking with the reliable sources you should then have established.

PART II

GOALS

"Part II is designed to help you begin to build the defenses needed for good personal security overseas. Remember, your primary goal is to develop a program that will make you as undesirable a target as possible. This is your best means of defense and the one over which you have the most control."

6
ANALYZING YOUR PERSONAL SECURITY SITUATION

How you use the next series of questions will largely depend on an analysis of your own overall personal security situation. If the threat in your area is serious and you are a potential target, you will probably want to consider all of the following information in detail. If the threat is not so serious and you are an unlikely target, then you need to concern yourself only with the major points. In either case you should carefully study all of the information in order to determine what will be applicable to your particular needs.

By the end of this section, you should know how to perform a threat, target, and situation analysis; how you can help keep yourself from becoming a target; what steps you can take in order to avoid an attack should you become a target; and how to handle an attack should one actually take place.

What is my "personal security situation"?

Your personal security situation is simply where you stand in terms of personal security, at the present time, in your particular location, and under the circumstances that exist there. A knowledge of that situation entails an understanding of what violent threats exist in your location, what your probability is of becoming a target of any of those threats, and a determination of your ability to reasonably defend yourself against these threats.

**Why is it important for me to analyze
my own personal security situation?**

You *must* analyze your own situation, if you hope to
defend your self and family in a reasonable manner. If you are
traveling to a very dangerous location you will want to know
why it is so dangerous, how you might be affected, and what
you can do about it. If you are assigned to a relatively safe area
you will also want to be able to plan accordingly, and not waste
a great deal of time and money on unnecessary security. In
essence, analyzing your personal security situation is the second
step you must take in developing your own personal security
program. The first step requires gathering the information
necessary for an adequate security analysis.

How should I analyze my personal security situation?

Analyzing your personal security situation may be easier
than you think. You need to perform a threat analysis, a target
analysis, and a situation analysis. What these three fancy terms
mean is that you must determine who in your location is capable of committing violent acts, who these people choose as their
victims, and what your capabilities are in regard to defending
yourself against these people. When you have the answers to
these questions you will have a fairly good idea about what
specific actions you should take to develop your own program.

How do I perform a threat, target, and situation analysis?

You perform a threat and target analysis by gathering the
necessary information from the sources described in chapter 5.
You perform a situation analysis by determining what reasonable and prudent measures you can take to defend yourself. I
have listed a series of questions relevant to each of the three
categories of analysis. By finding the answers to each of these
questions you will be able to perform an analysis of your own
personal security situation. The questions regarding your
situation analysis or your ability to defend yourself, will be
general in scope and are provided here only for familiarization.
A complete situation analysis can only be accomplished by
examining your specific defensive capabilities in detail, and
that subject is treated later in this book. Using the guidelines

that follow, complete to the best of your ability a threat and target analysis. Read the section marked "situation analysis" but do not attempt to complete it until finishing this book. Do not expect to be able to answer all the questions. It may simply not be possible, nor is it absolutely necessary.

THREAT ANALYSIS

A. What type of threat groups exist? Are they criminal or terrorist in nature?

B. Name the individual threat groups or elements in your area and answer the following questions about each one.

    1. How large is the group?

    2. What is the composition of group? Are the members students, communists, etc.?

    3. What type of threat does the group present? Do they commit assassinations, kidnappings, or bombings?

    4. How often do they commit these violent actions?

    5. Why do they use violence? What are their goals?

    6. How do they plan and operate? How do they hope to achieve their goals?

    7. How do they select their victims? Do they favor American victims?

    8. How long has the group used violent tactics? What recent acts has it committed?

C. What specific violent actions have been directed at Americans by any group, including criminals, in your host country during the last five years?

    1. If the attacks were successful, why were they successful?

    2. If the attacks failed, why did they fail?

D. What has the response by the local government been to the threat situation?

    1. What is the local government's attitude towards the threat situation?

    2. Does the local government have the capability to contain, diminish, or eliminate the threat situation?

    3. What specific actions has it taken to eliminate or reduce the threat situation?

      4. What specific actions has it taken to protect Americans?

E. What is the general political, economic, and social situation within the host country?

      1. Is the present government stable?

      2. Is the present government popular with a majority of the country?

      3. Does the present government have the support of major political groups and the military?

      4. Is the economy viable?

      5. Is there a large population of poor and uneducated people?

      6. Is there a history of mob action or social unrest?

      7. Are Americans liked or resented by the local population?

TARGET ANALYSIS

A. Based upon the threat analysis, am I as an American in danger from any local threat group?

      1. If so, what group and why?

      2. What is the type of their threat?

      3. What criteria are used by the group to pick the individual American target? Are they randomly selected?

B. Given my position, financial status, and profile within the community, am I more likely or less likely than any other American here to become a target of one of the violent groups?

C. Do I have any information that would make me believe that I am now or will be a probable target of one of the violent groups?

D. What are the specific characteristics about me or my family that may make me a potential target of a violent group?

SITUATION ANALYSIS

A. What is my probability of becoming a potential target of a violent group?

      1. How serious is the danger?

    2. Should I and my family remain in the country or should one or all of us leave?

    3. Psychologically, can I handle this danger or will it affect my work, family life, or health?

B. What can I do to reduce my target potential?

C. Can I effectively protect myself and my family from the potential danger?

D. What actions can I take to reduce my vulnerability to attack?

E. How much help can I expect to get regarding my security?

F. Will I need expensive security systems, guards, or armored cars and can I afford these things?

G. Will my personal security program need to be so involved as to encumber my style of living and enjoyment of the assignment?

H. What actions must I take to develop an effective security program which is relevant to the level of danger I face?

Special Considerations

Having completed these three analyses, you may find yourself in that small group of Americans who face a very serious level of personal danger in their prospective home abroad. If that is truly the case then you may need to either reconsider your overseas assignment, or be prepared to spend a considerable amount of money on a full-fledged security system similar to those provided high ranking diplomats and statesmen.

To better determine if you fall within this category, answer the following questions to the best of your ability:

    1. Are you by name or position known to be a definite target of any violent group and does that group presently possess the capability to launch an attack against you?

    2. Have you been informed by any office of the U.S. government that you are a target of a violent group and are in definite danger?

    3. Have you received a direct threat from a named violent group which has the present capability to launch an attack against you?

4. Have you been advised by the U.S. government that, due to the present conditions in your country of domicile, it can no longer be responsible for your safety?

5. Have you previously been the target of an intended attack by any violent group in your country of domicile?

A "yes" answer to any of these five questions will tend to confirm the seriousness of the threat you face. Under these conditions it is probably best that you leave the country at once, unless your company will underwrite the costs of your security program. In either case, sending your family home is probably called for as it will simplify your security problems and give you some peace of mind.

7
LOWERING
YOUR PROFILE

Basic Philosophy

Lowering your profile will be one of the keystones of your day-to-day personal security program. A low profile will definitely help you avoid becoming a target of the violent group(s) that may exist in your overseas location. It simply is what you do to make yourself less visible to the potential threat groups and thereby less likely to be even considered as a target. Most of these violent actions are directed at persons who serve directly or indirectly as political targets, or can be used as hostages to ransom large sums of money. In some cases, simply being an American citizen may put you in one of these groups. But generally, the threat group looks for one special person who best suits its political or economic needs and who, at the same time, has the *weakest personal security defenses*. Thus, even if the group has decided upon an American target it will try to choose the *one* American who *best* fits its needs. The fact is, they usually choose a high profile American who is visibly affluent in the local community, with close ties to the host country government, or who sympathizes with the host government's political or economic programs.

But how do these groups go about selecting that particular American who meets their target criteria? In a few cases, their selection relies on a sophisticated intelligence network, but in most cases they simply select from those individuals who are known publicly to fit one or more of their criteria. They depend upon the news media for targetting information, or on the common observance of the individual in the company of high government officials, or the affluent and rich lifestyle that the individual maintains. The bottom line is, targets are usually selected from that group of individuals who have a high public profile and are easily identified as persons who meet the group's targetting criteria.

Ultimately it is a method of common sense. Why *look* for a target when you already know a good one? Why should the violent elements spend a lot of time and effort doing something that has already been done for them by the high profile American?

While there are exceptions to the rule, most Americans can take measures to substantially lower their profile, reducing their risk of becoming targets. I know from experience, though, that some Americans will be unable to do this because of their official or business status. This group will have to compensate by increasing other security measures.

Profile reduction is achieved by avoiding the public lime-light. Basically this means you should do nothing to incite undue interest in your name, personality, or position.

Flamboyancy to any degree should play no part in your lifestyle, from the car you drive to the house you inhabit. Stay away from fancy accoutrements, whether flashy jewelry or garish clothes. It is safer to resemble the local middle class and to maintain a veneer as inconspicuous as possible. Attending society functions and jet set soirees paves a rapid road to trouble.

Your financial status is no one's business and your image should be one of understatement. Avoid ostentatious spending. Never keep large sums of money on your person, in your home, or in a local bank account. Your salary and position, and those of any associate or relative, are private matters.

Any contact with the media is a bad idea for people concerned with profile reduction. Therefore try to circumvent any social, business, or governmental affairs which might be covered by the press or photographers. Do not give interviews or public speeches. Interest-provoking entanglements—from personal relations to business deals—might attract undesirable attention.

Your past and present associations never should affect the inconspicuous facade so essential to overseas security. Examples of unmentionable topics include military, intelligence, and police service. Do not discuss locally unpopular U.S. corporations or controversial issues, and keep your opinions on the local government to yourself.

Maintaining inconspicuity is important for your company as well as your individual image. Help your company establish good employee and public relations, keeping the profile as low as possible given the demands of the business.

The "I am an American Syndrome"

The *I am an American* syndrome is perhaps the most serious flaw in the American personality in terms of vulnerability when living abroad. The vast majority of Americans living overseas suffers from this affliction. The location of their assignment or length of tour seems to have little affect upon the problem. This syndrome is symbolized by the average American's determined effort while living abroad to cherish all those things "American" and disdain all those things "foreign." This type of American will: try to live in an American enclave or compound; drive an American car; frequent clubs, restaurants, or bars that cater to Americans; send his children to American schools; socialize only with other Americans; have no local national he can really call his friend; know nothing of local history, customs, or culture; and probably speaks fewer than fifty words of the local language. In essence, he will try to create a little America in a foreign world and will cling to it with the tenacity of a bulldog.

The effect that this type of attitude produces in the local population is a redefining of the term *the ugly American*. The new ugly American is not rich or powerful. He just appears to his foreign hosts as someone who does not know anything about their country, does not even care to know anything, and can hardly wait to leave. Obviously, no American can expect this attitude to endear him to his new neighbors.

What this attitude has to do with lowering your profile is threefold: first, it completely isolates you from the local population, and even other foreigners, which makes you an easier target to identify. Second, it collectively produces an attitude in the local population that is adverse towards Americans in general. Third, it denies you information local contacts can provide. Further, this attitude lends support to violent elements who attack Americans in the name of furthering their just cause, regardless of what it might be.

No one can ask you to give up everything American simply on the grounds of security. It is not even advisable. However, you should make a determined effort to get to know your host country and its people, customs, and language, and try to treat your new country as a home, even if only a temporary one. It will not only help your security but will make your stay much more enjoyable and rewarding.

8
RESIDENTIAL SECURITY

Basic Philosphy

It has been said that a man's home is his castle. If this were literally the case, rather than a reference to legal rights, none of us would need to be too concerned about residential security. Just fill the moat and raise the drawbridge. Unfortunately, most of us cannot afford moats, drawbridges, or six-foot thick walls. Therefore we have to find other ways of making our homes secure.

Home security must play an important part of any personal security program. Your home is one of the few places where you can almost certainly be found during a known time period each day. If you *were* to become a target, your enemy would know where and when he has high odds of finding you. In addition, your home is the place where your family will spend most of its time and where you will go to rest and relax. For these reasons residential security is important not only from a general security standpoint but also from a psychological standpoint. It is the one place you do not want to have to worry about. So you should take the time to make your home as safe and secure as is reasonably possible. If you have to spend some of your own money on residential security, go ahead; you are not just buying good security, but peace of mind as well.

Your primary goal in home security is to provide yourself and your family with a comfortable, safe, and secure place to live. You must devote some of your time to making your home a place that is free of fear and anxiety, while your entire family

49

has both an understanding of all the security measures taken and a confidence in their ability to work.

If you are a potential target, you must remember that the security measures you take are not simply designed to stop a burglar, but rather are intended to defeat *any* attempt to attack you or your family in your home. This is an important distinction when you consider the stakes involved.

Maintaining good home security should always be a group effort. If you are single and live in an apartment this will not be a problem. But if you are single, live in a house by yourself, and are in a high threat environment, you may just have to get a roommate or some hired help. If you have a family then the problem is simple. Always ensure that everyone in your family, including your children, participates in the measures you take to obtain good home security. It is not just important for you but important for them.

Security Considerations for the Home

The following is an extensive discussion and listing of considerations and measures you may wish to incorporate into your residential security program. You will note that many of these items require your time and effort, rather than a lot of your money. While this is at least partially an effort on my part to provide you with measures which are affordable, it is also the most realistic approach in terms of good security. I know this from experience. In residential security, the best methods are often the cheapest and the simplest.

Selecting a Home

This is undoubtably the single most important action you can take to increase residential security. By selecting the right home, the right place to live, the best construction and location, you will be getting the maximum amount of benefit with the smallest amount of extra effort needed to make it secure. Consider the following points carefully when you make your choice and you will save yourself a lot of headaches:

LOCATION

Choose a good part of town. Not too posh but where the local middle or upper middle class lives. Make sure it is close to a police and fire station, or if possible, a military base. Make sure that schools, shopping, and health services are close by. If you plan to use public transportation it should come almost to your door. Avoid areas which are known to have high crime rates, vandalism, or are populated by radical, socialist, or communist elements. Choose a location which has several routes of travel to and from the main roads to your home. Look for the neighborhood which is considered safe by the local population; not just the American community. Try to live in an area where you have some friends. Live as close to work as possible.

Do *not* live in American enclaves or neighborhoods known to the local population as "foreign neighborhoods," unless those places are known to be secure or have been provided with extra protection. The same holds true for an isolated location; it may be charming but is probably very dangerous. If possible, choose a residence away from government offices or universities. You may be within walking distance of rioters or mobs near these places. Also avoid housing on dead end streets or cul-de-sacs. There is only one way out and someone may be waiting.

One final suggestion: do not live in any house whose previous tenant was a known target of any threat group. They may not know the target has moved!

TYPE OF DWELLING

Single family house: The single family house or detached house is often the first choice for Americans living abroad. This is especially true where the dollar still means something and where a nice house can mean a lifestyle unattainable to you in the States. Swimming pools, landscaping, maids' quarters, and fine architectural design are but a few of the possibilities you may encounter and which may be affordable if your employer provides you a housing allowance. Given the opportunity, this is what most of us will go for regardless of the security situation. After moving in we will begin to consider this aspect. Whether it is the best type of dwelling for your security needs can only be determined after you have completed your threat analysis and closely examined all the information in this chapter. In general the single family house is acceptable in the light to medium threat environment, assuming you spend the time and money to make it secure. In the high threat environment it can only be made safe at an expense that may be prohibitive to most Americans.

Townhouse: Like the single family unit, the townhouse is best judged in light of the threat analysis and after considering the related information in this chapter. Usually, the townhouse has some characteristics superior to the single family dwelling. Limited access, proximity of neighbors, and reduced costs for security hardware may all make the townhouse a superior choice over the single family dwelling. However, this is not necessarily the case. The usual high-density location of townhouses, their proximity to the street, and lack of garage or protected parking are but a few of the characteristics of townhouses which can make them a bad choice for your particular situation.

Apartment: In any high threat environment, an apartment will generally be your best choice, in terms of security, as a place to live. The great asset of the high rise apartment is that it is largely inaccessible from the outside due to its height above ground; and has extremely limited access, usually only one door. Thus, most of your security worries can be taken care of with a minimum amount of time, effort, and money. In most cases, an apartment can be made almost immune from break-in or forced entry and can provide you with security from virtually every type of attack. The drawback of an apartment from a security standpoint is the same as from a living standpoint. Because of the confined space and lack of a yard, you will tend to spend more time away from home in order to enjoy yourself, pursue your hobbies and interests, and keep your sanity. Since your level of security will probably drop considerably when you are away from home, this can be an important considertion.

Basic Specifications for Each Type of Dwelling

For the sake of expedience, this section will cover apartments and detached houses. Other types of dwellings can be considered by making appropriate use of the information in each section. After you have decided what type of dwelling you want to live in and have selected a general location or neighborhood, use the following guidelines in choosing your particular home.

HOUSES

Choose a solidly constructed house, made of brick, stone, concrete, or other hard, non-combustible material. Doors should be of solid construction, and fit snugly in their frames. Make sure the house has a good electrical system, capable of supporting added lighting and a burglar alarm system, should you need it. Avoid large, single pane windows (large enough that when broken a man can crawl through) unless they have bars or grille work. All ground floor windows should have bars or grilles.

Try to find a house surrounded by a high fence, or a sturdy wall that genuinely impedes access. Privacy is important. Make sure the house cannot be seen from the road or nearby houses or buildings. If possible, even the yard should be invisible to the passerby. However, the house should be within voice distance of the neighbors. Off road parking is a must, preferably in an enclosed garage with a private drive. If you plan to have a maid or chauffeur, select a house with specific accommodations for them. Keep in mind that the greater the degree of threat you face, the more time you will probably spend at home. Choose a comfortable house suitable to your family's needs.

APARTMENTS

Only consider apartments in buildings with security conscious management. Look for an apartment in a high rise building of solid, non-combustible construction. The best arrangement is a building raised off the ground by pillars, thus having no first floor. This limits access to one or two stairwells that will usually be attended. Your apartment building should have its own underground parking that is effectively restricted to tenants.

Access to the building itself should be restricted by both a desk clerk and a security guard. By living on a high floor, you will effectively limit access to only the apartment door. Make yourself difficult to observe with an apartment that does not face any other buildings in the near vicinity. An intercom system to the front door or desk is very desirable. If you have a balcony, make sure it is inaccessible from any other.

Improving Your Home's Security

With the above information in mind you should be able to decide *where* you should live, what *type* of dwelling you should live in, and make a selection as to the *particular* home you wish to rent or buy. What you must do now is decide what other measures you should take to make your new home even safer.

Limiting access is the key element to home security. If your enemy can't get in then he can't get to you. What you want to do is make it as difficult as possible for anyone to enter your home or even your yard. Obviously, you will not be able to stop a full scale military assault by a terrorist group using heavy weapons or bombs. You should not even try to. What you are trying to do is make entry into your home so difficult that only an extremely determined and forceful effort could hope to succeed.

DOORS

As stated before, all perimeter or exterior doors should be sturdy and of solid construction. Wood doors should be at least 1 3/4" thick, should not contain any glass, and should have a peephole or viewport. Metal doors should have a solid core and a peephole. French doors are only acceptable when they are not used in the main entrance and have very sturdy frames or have bars or grille work. Avoid sliding glass doors unless they are protected by bars or grille work. All exterior doors should be able to take the full force of one or two men ramming, kicking, or hitting them with a heavy object.

The door should fit snugly into the frame, and the frame itself should be both sturdy and solidly attached to the house. Door hinges are of considerable importance and should be located on the inside of the door. They should be solidly mounted to the frame and to the door itself. To avoid the possibility of someone removing the hinge pins and lifting the door out of its frame, all hinge pins should be of the non-removeable type.

Door locks are as important as the door itself. All exterior doors should have at least two good locking mechanisms on them and they should always be in use. Unless you are standing at or near the outside of your door it should *always* be locked. Whether you are in your house, just stepping next door, or going to the mailbox, lock your door. An unlocked door is an open invitation that will sooner or later be accepted.

The amount of information on locks that is worth discussing could take up the larger part of this book. So for the sake of brevity I will make some specific recommendations to fit most circumstances, and provide adequate protection for all but the most unusual situations. Additional reading on locks and/or consultation with a reputable locksmith is recommended.

All standard exterior doors should have at least one key-in-knob or mortised type lock and one vertical deadbolt lock. If you feel you need an additional lock it should be a surface mounted sliding deadblock. Each of these locks should be mounted at least one foot apart to reduce the chance of the door being jimmied open. *Strike plates*, which help defeat physical attacks on the locks, should be used as appropriate.

The *key-in-knob lock* should have a pin tumbler locking mechanism. The bolt portion of the lock should extend into the door jamb at least 5/8" or 3/4" preferably. The bolt portion of the lock should have a metal plunger on the trailing edge which serves to prevent the lock from being opened with a credit card or other piece of plastic. For this reason, another type of lock may be a better choice.

The *mortised lock* should be of the pin tumbler type and have a deadbolt which extends at least one inch into the door jamb. Ideally, the lock should be single cylinder and require a key on the outside, while having a thumb turn mechanism to unlock it from the inside. Double cylinder deadbolts require a key on both the inside and outside and should only be used on non-essential exterior doors that would not be used in event of fire, or when the door has glass panels.

The *vertical deadbolt* should have the pin tumbler locking mechanism and be single cylinder as stated above (note exceptions). Since the vertical deadbolt is mounted on both the door and the door frame it is very important that it be firmly attached in order to withstand efforts to break it away from its mounts.

The *surface mounted sliding deadbolt* will have the same characteristics as the vertical deadbolt except the bolt itself will lock in a horizontal manner and should extend at least 5/8" beyond the door's edge.

In more extreme circumstances you may want to install one final security device on your door. This lock system consists of a bar and bracket arrangement (Fort Apache style), with the bar stretching across the width of the door and fitting into brackets that are mounted in the door frame or wall on each side of the door. The bar itself should be made of steel and the brackets should be firmly bolted into the wall.

French doors should have the same type locks as described above except they should be of the double cylinder variety, requiring a key to open them from both sides. In addition, a locking bolt mechanism that mounts from each door into the floor or ceiling should be installed.

Dutch doors should have the same type locks as regular doors, with both doors having locks. They should also have two surface mounted throw bolts to secure the doors together when closed.

Sliding glass doors afford no protection against violent forced entry unless they are equipped with bars, steel shutters or a grille. These doors should have a key-type locking device with a hook-type bolt. Also, the door should have a good "charlie bar" or a key operated locking device that is mounted on the door track. Insure that the door fits snugly between both upper and lower running tracks, so it cannot be lifted or forced out of its frame.

Garage doors seldom offer adequate protection against violent attacks. Any existing garage door locks should be supplemented with at least one good internally mounted sliding deadbolt or padlock. However, in each case the door leading from your house to the garage should be treated as an exterior door and equipped with the same lock systems found on the front door.

WINDOWS

All windows should be of the frame type with multiple panes so that window breakage itself will not necessarily allow entrance. Unless you will be living in a relatively safe and crime-free environment, window bars, steel shutters or grilles are usually a must, at least on the ground floor. Window bars should be solidly attached to the exterior of the house in a fashion that will not allow their easy removal. The bars themselves should be of a vertical and horizontal pattern in order to preclude the use of a car jack to pry them apart. While many Americans may think that window bars are unsightly and overpowering, this is not the case overseas. In most parts of the world window bars are both common and necessary and come in numerous designs which are both effective and pleasing to the eye. You should also not be deterred by a fear of being caught in a fire with no way to escape. The doors of your residence should provide you with ample escape routes on the ground floor. Also, window bars or screens which can be released from the inside can be purchased for several windows of above ground floors, if necessary. Steel shutters are also a worthwhile consideration, especially if they can easily be opened and closed from the inside.

If you move into a house which does not have any of these protective features and you still feel you need them, then you should try to negotiate this with the lessor. The guarantee of a two- or three-year lease may inspire him to provide you with these features at his own expense. If he cannot pay at least make sure he will allow you to make these installations at your own or your employer's expense. Since you are adding to the value of his home he will seldom give you an argument.

All windows should have window locks. The variety of window locks are closely related to the variety of windows, their opening and closing characteristics, and how they lock firmly shut. The primary requisites for a window lock are that it be high quality, sturdy, firmly attached, and have a key type mechanism. On wooden or aluminum frame windows you can gain additional security by the use of drilled holes and a nail or screw. On a double hung wood window of this type you need only drill a hole through the frame of the upper and lower sash at the point where they overlap. Into this horizontal hole you then insert a nail which is smaller than the hole itself. The window is held shut by the nail and can be opened only after removing the nail and unlocking the lock. With the aluminum frame window you follow the same procedure, but use a screw rather than a nail and be sure that it can be removed easily.

A last note about windows. Aside from the threat they present as a means of forced entry into your home, the window can also be a deadly weapon. When broken or shattered by rocks, bullets, or a bomb blast the glass in the window will become tearing shrapnel, capable of causing both injury and death. An excellent means of preventing this is by applying safety film. This film is available from retail security outlets and can be applied to existing glass to prevent shattering or disintegration. Windows may also be replaced with Lexan, but this approach is considerably more expensive.

In either case, avoid letting your windows become view-ports for the rest of the world. Close your curtains at night and tilt venetian blinds during the day.

OTHER ENTRANCES

While windows and doors would seem to cover most of the entrances in American homes, they do not begin to touch on the variety of potential access ways that can be found in homes abroad. Coal chutes, ventilation shafts, large chimneys, and crawl spaces are just a few of the many types of entrances that can be found abroad. You should ensure that each one of these potential access ways is securely barred and locked.

In some cases, it may be more practical to permanently block some of these entrances. If this is the case, ensure that you have the landlord's permission before making these alterations and check to see if he will help pay for them.

One last note. Doggy doors may make your life easier but they are an absolute hazard in a threat environment. To the criminal mind they are an open invitation, no matter how small they may appear.

WALLS, FENCES, AND GATES

The purposes of walls, fences, and gates are threefold. First, they help prevent entrance to your yard and hence, your home. Second, they restrict or eliminate surveillance of your home by potential threat elements. Third, they act as a psychological barrier which tends to intimidate the intruder.

Walls and fences should be both sturdy and high to preclude visual surveillance. Gates should be sturdy and contain a key-type lock. The purpose of a wall or fence is not to stop a determined intruder, but rather to deter him and make his job more difficult. It can also help protect your children when in the yard and confine a dog, should you have one.

Some Points to Remember About Locks:

1. A lock is only good when it is used.
2. The quality of a lock can be partially determined by the amount of steel and brass it contains, and its relative expense.
3. Always change locks or key mechanisms when moving to a new home.
4. Always control your keys and never let more than one set of keys out, and then only to a trusted neighbor or friend. Despite what you may hear, no one has need of your keys but you. In an emergency the police can knock the door down.
5. Never "hide" keys near your door in case you forget them. Leave a set with your friend.
6. Never leave all your keys when having your car repaired. Leave only the keys absolutely necessary.
7. Never put any identification on your key chain. They are better forever lost than in the hands of the wrong person who will also have your address.
8. If you buy quality locks don't worry about them being picked. Few people can pick locks and even fewer will ever try.
9. When possible, order locks or cylinders which are specially made, use the same key, and have no master key.

10. Chain door locks should never be used. They serve only to view the visitor and can easily be defeated. Use a peephole instead.

11. Above all, know your locksmith. If he is trustworthy and honest he can be a real help. If he is not, your defense may be seriously weakened.

Other Deterrent Methods

LANDSCAPING

The landscaping of your yards and garden should allow you a clear view of your yard from your house. High shrubbery close to the home itself should be cleared away in order to eliminate hiding places for intruders. This is especially true around doors and other access ways. When possible, shrubbery or trees should be on the perimeter of your yard in order to shield you from outside observation.

LIGHTING

Outside lighting can be an important deterrent when used properly. It should emanate from the house (preferably from under the eaves) and be directed out towards the yard. It should clearly illuminate the sides of the house while at the same time providing general coverage of your yard. Generally, illumination that will reveal the movement of a man fifteen meters from the house is sufficient. You should also have separate porch, door, and garage lights. Also, make sure *outside fuse or electrical boxes are securely protected and locked.* Eliminating your electricity may be high on your enemy's list in order to make you more vulnerable and confused. When possible, all outside lighting should be activated by a photoelectric switch. (Note: If none of your neighbors uses outside lighting then you must consider the risk of possibly drawing attention to yourself).

DOGS

In addition to being man's best friend, a dog can be the most effective security item you can buy. He may also be one of the cheapest. He serves as both an alarm and a deterrent. He seldom needs repair or replacement, works indoor and outdoors, stands up to both the heat and the cold, is not dependent upon batteries or electricity, can distinguish between friend or stranger, and needs only a little food and affection to keep working twenty-four hours a day. In addition to all this he can deter, defend, and attack. There is not a security device or alarm on the market that can match those qualifications!

I firmly believe that no matter where you live oversea s or under what conditions, *a dog is an excellent investment.* While any type of dog will help, a larger dog is preferable. A trained attack dog might be an asset but is by no means necessary. In all probability your own dog or one that your children would choose for a pet will do just fine. You can either bring a dog with you from the States or purchase one locally. But check the expense of bringing one into the country, and local laws regarding quarantine or prohibition.

Apartment owners should keep their dogs in the apartment at all times when they are in the apartment themselves. Whenever the dog is let out of the apartment his owner should be with him. In this manner the dog is prevented from being poisoned or killed and at the same time is providing maximum protection to his owner. Remember, walking your dog should be done on a varying routine and in different locations, to avoid a predictable routine.

House dwellers should let their dogs roam in the yard during the day, and inside at night. If the dog ever shows signs of being poisoned, increase your vigilance because someone may have planned that action with a purpose.

GUARDS

Having a guard for your house may seem an extravagant measure in this country, but in many parts of the world it is both affordable and necessary. While guards in general will be covered in a later chapter, suffice it to say that if you can easily afford one, get one. Or better yet, get two. With a little effort to train them and obtain their loyalty they can be excellent additions to your residential security plan.

If you do decide to employ a guard, make sure you get the best one you can. Station him outside in the yard or with the children during the day and inside at night or during inclement weather. If you have more than one guard, keep one inside and one outside at all times. Allow them to switch duties but make sure this is not done on an exact schedule. Make sure they have only one set of keys, which must stay with the inside guard. Ensure that your guards fully understand your needs and are given explicit instructions. Always treat them in a professional manner. Periodically check to make sure they understand their instructions and are performing efficiently while on duty.

DOMESTICS
Like guards, domestics may not only be affordable but a necessity in numerous foreign countries. Moreover, they can be a godsend when it comes to home security. A good maid will know the neighborhood, the crime situation, how to identify suspicious people or situations, and a hundred other things that may be difficult for you to know or learn. Her knowledge and experience in the local situation can be an invaluable asset if put to the proper use.

Like maids, other types of domestics such as drivers, gardeners, and cooks can also perform the same role as a maid in regard to your security. What you must do is to make proper use of their knowledge and experience, provide them with precise and reasonable instructions, and obtain their loyalty.

The key to using domestics to supplement or enhance your home security is to verify from the beginning that they are honest and reliable. The way to ensure this is to check their criminal record with the local police (a common practice in most overseas countries), obtain a list of references and contact those references for verification, and have a personal interview with the prospective employee. If at all possible, employ domestics who previously worked for friends or associates. This can help save you time and offer further guarantees as to the domestic's integrity and character.

A final suggestion. You should consider hiring older domestics. They not only have more experience regarding home security, but are less likely to be secretly connected themselves with any terrorist or other violent element.

The Internal Safe Haven

The internal safe haven is simply a place within your house or apartment which is protected not only from the outside but from the rest of the house. It can take the form of a bedroom with additional locks on the door or can be a full-blown bunker in your basement. Its purpose is to protect you from a determined assault by persons who are intent on doing you harm and who may be able to enter your home by force. It serves no purpose outside of the personal security role.

In addition to providing you protection, the internal safe haven also acts as a command and control center. It is where you should store emergency food and water, keep a telephone and/or two-way radio, a first aid kit, flashlight, battery powered AM/FM radio, extra batteries, blankets, airhorn, and a gun.

While the classic safe haven is usually a room with reinforced walls and a steel reinforced door, other alternatives exist which can provide sufficient protection for most individuals, at a much lower cost. The best of these alternatives is the sleeping quarters "separator" door. This is simply a reinforced door which is built into the hallway separating the sleeping quarters from the rest of the house. It can also be mounted at the top of the stairs when the sleeping quarters are all upstairs. The primary purpose of this door is to keep an attacker who has entered the house from entering the area where you and your family are sleeping or seeking refuge. It will also allow you time to call the police or sound an alarm to get help. Above all, it will give you time, and time is the one factor your attacker has working against him.

The primary reason for putting this door in the hallway is that it can be locked while you are sleeping. Your whole family is afforded the same amount of protection without having to move to a specific location within the house. Most violent break-ins take place through exterior doorways rather than through windows. Your sleeping areas are thus an unlikely point of initial assault by the attacker. Perhaps the most useful aspect of this inner door is that it will ultimately tell you something about the intruder and his intentions. If the intruder attempts to break through the inner door there should be no doubt that he is an attacker and means you physical harm. So you will usually be safe to assume that drastic actions are appropriate.

For those of you who feel that a more sophisticated and secure safe haven is required in your situation, there are several further modifications you can make.

To begin with, walls, ceilings, and floor should be made of brick, block, stone, reinforced concrete, or a like material. Whatever you use it should be able to stop all small arms fire. It should also be substantial enough to prevent penetration by man-handled battering rams, sledge hammers, fire axes, and so on.

The door should be extremely sturdy and consist of reinforced steel planking, ½" thick. It should fit snugly into the frame and be secured with at least three heavy-duty hinges. The locks on the door may be of the same variety as those used on exterior doors, but must be augmented by steel blocking bars crossing the width of the door. The ends of the bars fit into brackets securely fastened into the wall on both sides of the door. Two of these bars should be sufficient. The best type of door is a safe door, especially when it is mounted into a steel frame embedded in reinforced concrete.

There should never be any windows in this room, and flammable material kept to a minimum. If air vents are necessary, be sure they are made of steel piping with a fan apparatus to force the air in and out. There must also be a blocking device on the piping to preclude tear gas or other agents from being pumped in.

Without doubt, very strong internal safe havens have their place in the residential security role for some people and families. For most Americans residing abroad, a reasonable variation of the safe haven is a good idea because it provides some additional protection and can act as a command and control center for the family. In most cases the fully equipped safe haven should be considered only by those in an area where civil disturbances or a total breakdown of law and order may occur or has occurred.

Alarms and Warning Devices

The most important thing to know about alarms and warning devices is that they do not directly stop anyone from entering your home. Alarms can only *deter* intruders by warning them that their presence has been detected. Alarms can play an important role in deterring burglars but are not nearly as effective with people intent on causing you physical harm. Before you buy or install any burglar alarm or warning device make sure you have taken all the other suggestions in this chapter to make your home secure. (The one exception to this is smoke and fire detectors, which you should absolutely include in your home. They are cheap, efficient, and can save your life.)

Probably the most important feature of alarm systems is the "time problem" they present to the intruder. If the potential intruder realizes you have an alarm system (and if you have one you should make sure the fact is posted on your home's doors and windows), he is faced with the problem of completing his attack quickly enough to allow for his successful escape. Shortly after he enters your home, the alarm system will announce his presence not only to you but to neighbors and hopefully the police. This will make his planning more difficult and may persuade him to choose an easier target, which is certainly the goal from your viewpoint. Unfortunately, most violent elements intent on attacking you in your home will not be prevented from doing so by alarm systems, as the very nature of their planned actions will necessarily be loud and attract attention.

All in all, alarm systems represent a mixed bag in regard to protecting residences from the various threat elements. The best approach is as follows: if you can easily afford a system or can get your employer to pay for one, then by all means get the best system available. But whatever you do, remember: the best alarm system in the world presents no physical barrier. It is a warning system, a psychological barrier, and a means of calling for help. It may supplement your bars, locks, and barriers, but never think an alarm can supplant them.

Choosing an Alarm System

Many types of alarm systems are available for residences, and technological advances in this field are almost a daily occurrence. The basic types of systems consist of door and window contacts, pressure mats, motion detectors, sound detectors, vibration detectors, and photoelectric sensors. While all of these systems have their pros and cons, the door and window contact or switch sensors are the most logical in terms of personal security because they warn you that someone is attempting to enter your house, rather than informing you that someone is already inside. These sensors should be installed on all doors, windows, and exterior access ways which might afford entry to a man.

Regardless of what alarm you choose, a few points should be considered for any system to be employed overseas. The system should consist of three major components: a detection apparatus, a control unit, and an alarm. A good system will also feature a fail-safe mechanism that allows you to test the system periodically, and an anti-neutralization feature which will keep the system from being disarmed. The system's control unit should be disguised, concealed, or hidden.

Buy an Underwriters' Laboratory approved system, if American made. The alarm should operate on the local electrical current and have a battery backup, or be completely run on batteries. Make sure the system is easy to install and repair, and covered by guarantee or warranty. A time delay feature is necessary, which allows you to arm and disarm the system without setting it off.

The alarm system should work comfortably around your lifestyle without creating unnecessary burdens or unusual requirements.

Additional information on many aspects of residential

security can be obtained free by writing: The Consumer Information Center, Pueblo, Colorado 81009.

The Telephone

Everyone in your household, including children and servants, should be instructed on proper and secure methods of handling telephone calls. The telephone call is commonly used by threat elements to obtain information about you and your family, your presence at home, and other information regarding your vulnerabilities.

Always try to obtain an unpublished and unlisted number, and consider that your phone may be tapped. Never identify yourself upon answering the phone. Instead, wait for the caller to ask for you by name, and do not identify yourself to a stranger. If the caller appears to have a wrong number, ask him to tell you what number he is calling and instruct him to try again. Do not give him your number or name.

Keep a log of any unusual calls and see if they represent any kind of pattern. Make notes regarding time, nature of inquiry, apparent sex and age of caller, voice characteristics, and other distinctions.

If you receive several calls from strangers asking for a family member who is not at home or who is away on business, LIE! Tell the stranger that the person is there but indisposed. Get a number where the call may be returned and call the number yourself to verify its validity.

Inform the police immediately if you receive any threatening calls. Beware of calls or visits reporting a family member of friend's injury or accident. Check the information before you report to the scene or hospital.

Remember, in most parts of the world today the phone systems are antiquated compared to our own. Consequently wrong numbers are common and should not be cause for undue alarm. But no matter how innocent the caller may appear, practice good telephone security and watch for signs that someone is trying to obtain information about your personal security program.

Always keep a list of emergency numbers next to the phone and learn enough of the local language to be able to make an emergency phone call.

Countering External Surveillance

Countering external surveillance is perhaps the single best way to protect yourself, family, and home from a violent action. Almost no attempt to assassinate, kidnap, or bomb you at home will be made without a thorough surveillance of your home and the activities taking place there. Any attempted violence will ordinarily be preceded by surveillance used to gather information about your daily routine, the household's routine, your residence itself, and the security precautions you have taken. In fact, efforts to attack you in your car will normally be preceded by surveillance of your home, your departure times, your make of car, and your initial routes from home to work and the store. Thus it is extremely important that you identify surveillance of your home as soon as it has begun.

Surveillance of your home can take many forms. You are probably aware of some of them already, but here are some hints at what you, your family, and domestics should look for.

Be aware of strangers, whether they are walking, driving around the neighborhood repetitiously, or simply sitting in a parked car, van, or truck. Be suspicious of anyone requesting information or trying to start conversations with you, family members, or domestics. Pay close attention to workmen or peddlers near your home. Check out telephone repairmen, utility workers, and other workmen by calling their local office. When making notes of suspicious people or occurrences, gather as much data as possible: descriptions, frequencies, license numbers, date and time, and patterns.

Monitor nearby vacant houses or apartments which may be used as surveillance stations.

Avoid putting any personal or descriptive material into your garbage. To the right person it will read like a book.

If you feel that you may be under surveillance, contact the police or other appropriate authorities immediately. In most cases, if a threat group feels its surveillance has been detected and the authorities informed, it will immediately change or cancel its plans.

Access: Who, When, and Where

Access to your home should always be limited to those people you know personally or can identify prior to their gaining entrance. There are a hundred logical sounding explanations that a stranger can use to gain entry to your house. None of them are even good enough for you to open the door until you have verified an absolute need and corroborated the identity of the individual. Whether it is a policeman, repairman, utility man, real estate agent or other plausible sounding caller, you should first ask for identification, to be slipped under the door, then call their local office for verification. If a stranger needs to borrow your phone due to a car breakdown, make the call for him. Above all, do not let the stranger in. Be suspicious and use your head. Again, make sure everyone in your household is instructed in this area and follows your specific guidelines.

Bomb Detection and Handling

There is a myriad of information available on bomb detection and handling. Most of it is not only useless but dangerous to the average person or family. You do not attempt to detect a bomb itself but rather an object, package, or piece of mail that could conceal a bomb. Neither you nor your family should ever handle a bomb or a suspect bomb. That is a job for experts and even they get killed doing their job.

Detecting a bomb, or rather its packaging, will be made much easier if you have done a good threat analysis. Your threat analysis should tell you the frequency of bombing attacks against Americans, the type of bombs used, the type of packaging used to conceal the bomb, and where most bombing attacks take place. With at least some knowledge of these facts you will be in a better position to judge the threat to yourself and your family and know what you should be aware of and what you should be looking for.

Start this phase of your security program by *never* accepting packages without a return address or from someone you do not know. Handle letters in the same manner. Always check letters for metal or stiff objects other than paper before opening them and never open any letter containing this or any other type of unusual object or material. Along these same lines, check packages and letters for correct spelling and good grammar. Make sure the handwriting is clear and legible. Defects in these areas may indicate a lack of authenticity and possibly a bomb.

If you feel you must admit a stranger to your house always stay close by him. If he is a repairman, make sure he takes everything with him when he leaves. Never let him go for lunch and leave a toolbox or other box or bag behind. The same holds true for purses, briefcases, and other similar articles left in your home by anyone other than trusted friends or associates. Boxes, packages, bags, or garbage left mysteriously near the walls of your home are cause for similar alarm.

All members of the household should be instructed on handling telephoned bomb threats. They should remain calm and composed and try to find out: 1) when the bomb is set to go off; 2) what type of bomb it is; 3) where the bomb is located; 4) who is calling and how they can be reached.

If you do suspect any object may be a bomb, evacuate the area immediately and then call the authorities.

Absence from Your Home

In an overseas situation, absence from your home is best handled by leaving someone behind. This may be a friend, domestic, or guard. In any case, your home security is best protected by having an individual stay in your home while you are away. If this is not possible, then there are several precautions you can take to increase the security of your home while you are away. Start by making certain that all deliveries are cut off (newspapers, mail, etc.). Use automatic timers or photoelectric switches to turn lights off and on. (Twenty-four-hour timers with variable settings and multiple hookups are best.) Ask a neighbor to check the premises, pull the drapes open and closed, park his car in your drive, or keep your yard up. Never leave a light on twenty-four hours a day or keep your drapes permanently closed. Never advertise the fact that you will be away. Only your neighbors and a trusted friend should know this. If applicable, ask the local police to check your house occasionally.

When you return, use caution before entering your home. Check for signs of forced entry or unusual activity. If things do not look quite right, go to a telephone away from your home and call the police.

Varied Routines

Predictable routines are the nectar of the threat element. Avoid routines as much as possible and ensure that your family does the same. I cannot stress this point enough. So leave for, and return from work at varying times. Have your spouse shop at different times on different days. Avoid going to a club or dinner on the same night each week. Never establish any routine that puts you in your yard or outside your apartment at a certain time each day or night. This includes walks, taking the dog out, reading the paper on the patio or balcony, or even playing ball with the kids. Make your lifestyle at home as unpredictable as possible without causing undue stress on your family.

Car to Door Security

Car to door security is a very important part of your residential security plan. The bulk of car to door security considerations will be covered in chapter 10. Meanwhile, it is important that you remember that your residence is one of the few places where you will be able to carefully plan your car to door security routine, and many kidnappings and assassinations take place between these two points.

Residential Security: How Much Is Enough?

The answer to this question will depend largely upon you. Unless you have an expert to give you personal advice, you will have to decide just how far to carry the recommendations I have made. If you have done a good threat analysis you should have a good idea of what you are up against, and just how secure your home needs to be for adequate protection. Try to make it as secure as you feel necessary. Make your adjustments based on the facts. Follow all the basic guidelines in this chapter and make sure your family participates. Neither underestimate the potential threat nor become paranoid about it. If you have done a good job you probably have very little to worry about. So follow your home security plan and enjoy your new home.

9
OFFICE SECURITY

Any good personal security plan must take into account the security of your office or other working environment. Fortunately, good personal security is usually achieved more easily in the working environment than at home. Furthermore, many readers may have the added benefit of having someone specifically charged with ensuring a safe and secure working environment for you and your fellow employees. Security officers, or specialists, are commonly found in military, governmental, and large corporate offices overseas. In areas of major U.S. presence it is not uncommon to find foreign government security forces provided specifically for the protection of the U.S. citizens. However, some Americans have to go it alone for one reason or another. In either case your direct involvement and concern in the security of your working environment is an important determinant of your overall safety.

Since it is not possible to cover all the various working environments Americans may encounter overseas, this chapter will concentrate on the one environment that is most common to Americans overseas and has traditionally been the most popular target of the various threat groups: the business or government office.

The Office and the Company: a Special Situation

Your place of work and your business or governmental affiliation may pose a special threat that must be carefully considered. Many threat groups select targets based upon the individual's employment with a specific company or government agency. This is especially true of urban guerrilla and revolutionary groups, who often try to attach political significance to their acts of violence. If you are a U.S. government employee in a country where radical elements adversely propagandize the local government's close association with the United States, you may be a prime target. Employment with a major U.S. corporation in a third world or underdeveloped country can also cast both you and your company in the role of an "exploiter of the people." There are numerous other situations that have similar implications. Suffice it to say that simple affiliation with a particular business or government agency can make you the impersonal target of a number of threat groups.

The above has special relevance to the problem of office security. Many groups will prefer to undertake their violent actions against you while you are in your employer's offices. This lends credence to their claim that they are fighting oppression (represented, in their eyes, by your employer), rather than choosing randomly selected targets. While often true with urban guerrillas and revolutionary groups, this is almost always the case with radical religious, social, political groups that tend to use violence only during demonstrations, marches, and calculated mob actions. The burning and destruction of American business and government offices by mobs or rioters is all too common.

The special problem that results from all of this is that virtually any American can become a target simply by his presence in the offices of an American firm, or by his employment with that agency. A potential target does not necessarily have to be a high level executive or even a low ranking manager. The fact that you are an American and work for an American employer may be quite sufficient in a terrorist's mind. So pay special attention to your security at work, and consider your employer's profile carefully when you do your threat analysis.

Although this chapter concentrates on the problems of office security, extrapolation of this information to other work environments can help you adapt it to whatever your particular work situation may be. Consider the information carefully and refer back to the chapter on residential security for a more thorough explanation of security measures that are applicable to both situations.

Office Location

Offices are best located in the central business district of the better part of town. Unlike residences, do not hesitate to locate your office in an expensive or high rent area. They generally have better security and are given more consideration by the police.

Rent offices on upper floors. Never rent a whole building. Burning it down will hurt only you and the owner; not other local businesses. Locate your offices on a main street or busy thoroughfare. Do not locate too close to universities or government buildings except police and military barracks. The idea is to avoid becoming a target conveniently located for demonstrators gathered for some other purpose.

Choice of Office Buildings

Choose a modern building that is essentially fireproof. Try to avoid buildings which have a substantial amount of glass. Instead, look for an office with a nominal number of tinted windows, or one where the manager will allow you to apply privacy or anti-shatter tape to your windows. When possible, select a building that does not directly face an adjacent building, in order to deter surveillance. Make sure the building has a good security force and that the other tenants are also security conscious. Before signing any lease, make certain that the manager will let you make reasonable alterations which may later become necessary to enhance your security. Check to see that the building has a good anti-fire sprinkler system. Your office building should also have underground or private parking for tenants and employees.

When possible, rent an entire floor and hire your own security personnel to monitor elevators, doors, and visitors.

Adding to Your Office's Security

Beef up your doors as necessary, and ensure that your windows can be locked. Always install good quality, new locks on your office doors and maintain strict key control. Never use electronic combination door locks if you have local employees. Permanently lock all doors leading to hallways, elevators, and other access routes except those that are absolutely necessary.

When possible, use only one door to enter offices on any given floor. If you must take up several floors, install stairs inside the office that lead up or down as appropriate. Always use a two-door anteroom system for main entrances. Here install a view-port, bulletproof glass, or a closed circuit television system outside the main door to allow you to observe any visitors before they enter the office. Hallways, stairs, and common areas must be well lighted and patrolled by security personnel. When necessary to the potential threat, establish a safe haven within the office complex.

Alarms and Warning Devices

When appropriate, install alarms or warning devices in your offices even if the building is already equipped with such systems. If the building does not have a good fire or smoke detection system, install one in your offices. Also make sure that you have a good evacuation plan.

Telephones

Make sure all office personnel practice good telephone security. They should never give out any information on any employee other than to state that he is in or out. They should not state what time any employee might be expected to leave or return. All employees should be briefed and drilled on handling bomb threats and other violent threats against the offices or its employees.

All employees should be able to handle bomb threats themselves, without the aid of another employee or superior. They must also learn to remain as calm and composed as possible.

The employee should attempt to extract the following information from the caller, in the order given:

- When is the bomb set to go off?
- What type of bomb is it?
- Where is the bomb located?
- Who is calling, and how can they be reached?

When possible the employee should attempt to keep the caller on the line as long as possible and learn as much of the following as possible:

- Caller's approximate age and nationality.
- Caller's accent and fluency.
- Helpful background noises as may be appropriate.
- Name of group or person taking credit for the bombing.
- Reasons for bomb being planted.
- Whether additional bombings can be expected.

Bomb Detection and Emergency Planning

Since bombings statistically represent one of the largest threats to American offices overseas, it is imperative your offices have a bomb detection and emergency evacuation plan. Of the two, the emergency evacuation plan is the most important. It may be similar to a standard fire evacuation plan, but should take into consideration the possibility that the terrorists want you to evacuate. Here a greater danger may await you and your fellow employees once outside your offices. Thus, a primary prerequisite is that all employees be evacuated to an area that is known to be both safe and secure, and not just onto the street. Police should be notified of the bomb threat simultaneous to the evacuation. Upon arrival they should be told where the employees are located, and requested to provide police protection until the incident is over.

Your bomb detection plan should be defensive in nature. It should include careful inspection of all visitors and their packages, immediate reporting of any suspicious objects around the office, a thorough inspection of all mail prior to opening, and special instructions to personnel who open mail. Every employee should be assigned a specific area to cover, both on a daily basis and in the event of a bomb threat. These areas should be next to their normal working areas, which they will be best familiar with. Instruct each employee to inspect their areas upon arrival in the morning and before departure at night. Obviously, all areas should be kept free of packages, loose materials, or clutter that would make an unusual package more difficult to detect quickly.

In the event of a bomb threat, all employees should make a quick scan of their assigned areas and report any suspicious object, without touching it. That work is for the police and the bomb experts. No employee who searches extensively or attempts to move or dismantle a bomb can be considered anything but stupid. Employees who are members of a trained company "search team" will naturally handle bomb threats in a different manner than previously described.

Office Access

To the degree possible, access to the office should be limited to employees and visitors who are both known and have previous appointments. All other visitors should be carefully screened and their identities verified prior to entry. Mail, deliveries, and maintenance should be handled in the same manner.

Cleaning crews represent a serious problem to office security since they often have their own keys, work unwatched at night, and have access to all parts of the office. Make certain that these people are carefully screened by the building management. When possible, arrange for the same people to clean your office each day. While this will be helpful, it is not really a solution. The best possible approach, and the only realistic one in high threat areas, is to hire your own janitors and check them out yourself. In addition, it is best to have them do their work during the day when the office staff can be around to watch them. This may be a small inconvenience, but the security benefits are well worth it.

If you have a large office suite or complex you should consider using internal checkpoints. This can be accomplished with ease by simply closing doors between office suites and locking them. A secretary can be assigned to monitor the door and open it to verified employees or visitors. These locked doors must not interfere with office evacuation plans.

Countering External Surveillance

Instruct all employees to make note of any possible surveillance of the office or its occupants. Persons loitering in halls, lobbies, or stairways, suspicious visitors, frequent passersby, and so forth, should all be reported to the building security office and a log kept. Where applicable, employees should be on the alert for surveillance from the street or adjacent buildings. A close watch of employee parking areas is important if the area is not supervised by security personnel.

GENERAL OFFICE SECURITY GUIDELINES

All employees should be fully briefed on the security plans and procedures used in the office. Keep everyone there informed of any situations that may affect their security.

The office should maintain an emergency medical record for each employee. It should also maintain notification and procedure instructions for each employee in the event of an emergency, such as kidnapping.

During times of high threat or danger the office staff should remain home or, if absolutely necessary, be comprised of a volunteer skeleton crew. This is also important on local holidays or other symbolic days when a prevailing calm may give way to high tensions and anger. Terrorist attacks, riots, and mob actions often occur on specific days which have a symbolic meaning to the particular group. You may obtain this information from the U.S. embassy security officer.

Employees should be encouraged to participate actively in the office's security. Hold periodic, informal security discussions to give employees a chance to make recommendations and discuss problem areas.

Office management, for their part, should maintain a close and cordial relationship with local police and other authorities responsible for their security.

If the office has a security officer, he should be treated as a member of the business team and not left alone in some remote corner of the office. He should work with regular employees and be included in all standard business meetings. His job may be as important to the profit margin as the chief tax accountant's.

10
CAR SECURITY AND DEFENSIVE DRIVING

For those who will live in an environment where kidnappings, assassinations, malicious woundings, and extortion are regular fare, the information in this chapter will be of special importance. The defensive techniques described should not only be committed to memory; they must become an integral part of your daily life. The reason for this is simple: over 80% of all kidnapping and assassination attempts by terrorist elements in recent years have taken place while the target is either in his car, or going to or from his car. Only slightly less dangerous are your other regular and predictable trips by foot from your home or office to a nearby store or restaurant. Security for these trips is just as important as for a trip in your car.

The basic problem with maintaining your security while going to or from your car, or while you are in it, is that *most of the advantages lie with the attacker*. An attacker can choose the time, place, and mode of attack, and may be able to surprise you. Therefore you must make every use of the few advantages afforded you to optimize your chances. While your best effort may not provide you with total security, it will substantially add to your security and diminish your risk, even if only in a relative way. It is important to remember that your primary goal is to achieve a level of security that will make you a difficult target, and thus encourage the potential attacker to select an easier target. Your ability to evade, escape, or defeat an attack is secondary to that goal.

The Prime Advantages

There are three prime advantages you will have over your attacker and they are the bulwark of everything to follow. If you remember nothing else, remember these:

1. By practicing good automobile security, driving security, and to-and-from car security, you may make the potential attacker's job so difficult he may either give up his plans or choose someone else as his target.

2. By recognizing surveillance or other suspicious occurrences you can learn that you may be the target of a forthcoming attack and take appropriate actions to eliminate that possibility.

3. By recognizing that an attack is about to take place, or is beginning, you can take specific defensive or offensive measures to thwart the attack and escape.

The reason that these three points are so important is that they represent the pendulum of security in this area. If you take full advantage of them you will maximize your prospects of surviving. If you dismiss the three you will so seriously diminish your security that, should you become a target, you will almost certainly be on the losing side.

The Disadvantages

To better understand what you are up against, we must look at your situation from the terrorist's point of view. Once the terrorist has selected you as a potential target, he will take at least three more steps. First, operatives will gather as much information about you as possible in order to determine your real value as a target (potential money from kidnapping, embarrassment to local government or flight of foreign business in the event of your assassination and so forth). Second, the terrorist will study your security defenses to see if an attack can be successful without undue effort or risk. Third, your weakest security point will be extensively studied to learn how this weakness can best be exploited in an attack.

Assuming you have passed the first two points of his screening process, it is the third that becomes the most important. The third point, your weakest point of security, will ordinarily be the time when you are going to or from your car, or while you are driving. From the terrorists' point of view this is often the most promising time to attack, since at this point the target has few built-in defenses, can be attacked on neutral ground, and is easily identified. Surveillance is also more easily accomplished when the target is in his car. Further, the target can be isolated, and the attack made at the time and place of the attacker's choice with most contingencies taken into account. This allows the attack to be made quickly and with the greatest element of surprise, permitting quick escape via a number of possible escape routes as well. Whether successful or not, this type of attack usually gains wide media coverage for the attacker, and thus propagandizes his organization.

Countermeasures: to and from Your Car

The importance of getting safely to and from your car cannot be overestimated. Most of you will have to do this alone, without any tangible means of protection, and often in the dark. Your only defense may be your knowledge of security countermeasures, your quick thinking, and your ability to use good judgement and make decisions. Unfortunately, I can only help you with the countermeasures. The rest is up to you.

There are four precautions you should take every time you are in transit to or from some place to your car. Practice them and they will become automatic.

1. Choose the safest route possible.
2. Detour from any suspicious person or situation.
3. Watch for surveillance without being obvious.
4. Be mentally prepared to act should an attack take place.

TRANSIT SECURITY GUIDELINES

The following suggestions will help you act upon these four points. When preparing to leave your house, carefully survey your yard for anyone who might be hidden. For ten minutes before leaving, check for any unusual people or activities near your house, yard, or on the street. Look for workmen, vendors, people sitting in parked cars, and so on. Do not leave if things look suspicious to you. Use the phone to check out workers and utility crews by verifying their assigned location with their company management. Ask a neighbor or have one of your domestics check out peddlers and vendors. Persons in parked cars, loiterers, and other suspicious persons should be checked out by the police.

When leaving your apartment, check the peephole to make sure no one is outside your door. Step outside the door and check the hallway to make sure it is clear of any suspicious persons.

Proceed directly to the elevator or main stairway. Use stairs only when an elevator is not present in the building. Do not enter any elevator that is being held for you by anyone you do not know. Never enter an elevator occupied by a suspicious person. Try to make sure that *you* punch the button for the floor you want. When it must be done for you, check that the proper button is pushed. When in an elevator occupied by persons other than yourself, stand near the emergency button.

Carefully check the lobby and note suspicious persons or activities. See if anyone follows you when you leave. Before leaving the building, survey the adjacent street and sidewalks. If warranted check out suspicious persons or activities with authorities before leaving the building.

If you use a garage or underground parking, look over the area carefully before proceeding to your car from the elevator or stairs. Do not use underground parking if it is unattended or unsecured.

Choose the safest route to your car, rather than the most direct. If you park some distance from your apartment building, try to vary your route from the building to the car and vice versa. Once again, look for people following you on the way to your car. If you think you are being surveilled, do not go to your car. Enter a nearby building or store immediately and call a cab, or if warranted, the police.

When you arrive at your car, get in quickly and lock the door. Start the car immediately and be prepared to drive away quickly.

When leaving your office or a frequently visited store, restaurant, or club, use these same security precautions.

Remember, you are primarily looking for surveillance. It is the usual predecessor of a terrorist attack and will likely occur several times before an attack takes place. If you are more worried about a violent criminal attack, you must assume that any surveillance may mean an attack is imminent. Act accordingly.

Always park as close to your destination as possible, but vary your location and walking routes to and from your destination. Switch cars, use taxis, and car pool on a varying schedule.

When taking a cab, always remain indoors and call a cab by phone or have the doorman call one. Use cabs only from reputable companies. Never take a cab which is obviously waiting "just for you" without having been summoned. Never take a cab which has been parked down the street and pulls out only when you reach the sidewalk. If you have any doubts, never take the first cab that stops. Wait and take the next one.

Car Security

Good car security entails the selection, modification, maintenance, and inspection of the car(s) you will use during your overseas tour. Your primary purpose will be to provide yourself with a car that has a low profile, good protection from tampering or break-in attempts, excellent defensive driving characteristics, and essential security options. A few of you in high threat areas, where terrorists are active and target Americans with your profile, may need fully armored cars. That subject will be covered in a later chapter. For those who do not face such a direct threat, it is important that you get as much security out of your car as you possibly can without going to exceptional expense. While that may sound like a large order, it is in fact fairly easy. What it requires on your part is a decision to purchase a car which meets your security needs, rather than simply your esthetic taste.

Begin by considering the kind of car you will need and the options it should have. This kind of car can generally be purchased from a local dealer in the host country and will require only a few options which he may not be able to supply. If this is the case, you can buy the optional equipment from parts and accessories stores or, if necessary, from a mail order house.

The type of car you choose may vary, but by all means do not purchase a sports or luxury car. Pick a crashworthy car model commonly seen in your new location that is plainly painted, without special emblems or license plates. All this will help keep your vehicle profile low, while fitting in with the crowd.

CAR OPTIONS

Here is a list of optional equipment that your automobile should have, in my opinion:

- Optional higher powered engine, if offered, to help make your escape.
- Below surface, smooth door locks, for security from entry.
- Trunk and hood locks, to make it harder to find a place to put a bomb or disable the car.
- Locking gas cap, to prevent sabotage.
- Dual side mirrors with remote control, to check for surveillance.
- Power steering, for quick and easy handling.
- Air-conditioning, so there is no need to roll down windows.
- Power disc brakes, for emergency stops.
- Steel belted radial tires, for better handling.
- Rear window defroster, if applicable, so you can use your inside mirror to watch for surveillance.
- Heavy-duty suspension, for rough road conditions.
- Heavy-duty or reinforced front and rear bumpers, for ramming or being rammed.
- Under hood mounted siren or foghorn, to surprise your attackers and call for help.
- First aid kit, fire extinguisher, and an emergency kit

containing flares, flashlight, tools, canned food, water, and blankets.

- Seat belts and shoulder harnesses for all occupants, for general safety and to keep you in your seat during violent maneuvering.

The following car options are worth considering if the threat situation is significant and if you can afford them:

- High intensity headlights to see farther at night and give you added time to react.
- High intensity backup lights.
- A communication system, but no external antenna other than AM/FM radio, to report detours, delays, and call for help.
- Grille mounted police or flasher lights for surprise and escape.
- Anti-theft or tamper alarm to keep a bomb from being installed.
- Remote ignition starting system so the car can warm up without you being in it, and to check for ignition wired bombs.
- A complete solid seal undercarriage cover panel, to keep bombs from being attached to the undercarriage.
- Timed lighting system, so you can see your way to the door.
- Heavy-duty battery and ignition system so your car starts quickly, and every time.

After you have purchased your car and added the options appropriate to your particular situation, you must maintain it in top condition. This may seem a bit obvious since most of you always keep your car in good condition without really giving it a second thought. That is fairly easy to do in the States, but it can be much more difficult in some areas of the world. Car maintenance can be so time consuming and costly that even minor tune-ups are forever postponed. Do not let this happen. Your car must not only be maintained for highway safety, but also for emergency purposes and defensive driving.

Periodically check to ensure that your special systems or options are working according to specifications. Keep your car clean and washed. This will come in handy when inspecting for tampering or bombs. Always keep at least one-fourth tank of gas in the car. All-night gas stations are a myth in some countries and you never know when you might have an emergency.

Car inspection is necessary to ensure that your car has neither been tampered with nor has it had a bomb placed in it. Signs that someone tampered with your car generally indicate that someone was trying to steal ornaments or parts, or the car itself. Another possibility is that someone was trying to get into your car to gather information about you. Tampering can also indicate that someone was trying to mark your car for surveillance by means of reflector tape on the fender, chalk marks on tires, and so on. The last, and most serious possibility, is that someone was trying to put a bomb in your car.

The reason for inspecting your car carefully each time before using it is to ensure that someone was only *trying* to do one of these things, rather than actually *did* do it.

For most of you this car inspection need not be an elaborate process, but rather can be performed while walking quickly around your car. The chances are slim that you will need to worry about a car bomb. This is very fortunate since it can take a professional an entire day to do a good bomb search on a car. Car bombing is a fairly elaborate and difficult way of simply murdering someone and is generally uncommon overseas. In any event your threat analysis should tell you if this should be a particular concern. Breaking into your car to gather information on you, or marking your car for surveillance is another story. These are telltale signs that someone is very interested in you and the chances are that someone is up to no good. In fact, marking your car may not only mean you are being surveilled but that an attack is imminent. The reason for marking your car prior to an attack is to make it easier for those people who may be waiting for you, rather than those following you, to identify you positively as their target. That may be no small feat if you are driving a small car widely used in the country.

Tampering is a sign of interest. Try to determine exactly what that interest is. If someone has been in your car but has not stolen anything, he may be gathering information. Keep your guard up and look for other signs that you may have become of interest to a threat element. If someone appears to have marked your car (reflecting tape, chalk on tires, spray paint), then take a different route home and try to determine if you are being surveilled. Carefully consider your situation and try to determine if you may have become a target of some threat element. Lastly, if you find a bomb on your car, it will be apparent that you are a target. You should get police protection immediately. If such protection is not available, then you will have to call in professional help in order to maintain a much higher level of security. It may also be time to request reassignment to another area.

THE CAR SEARCH

An efficient yet quick car search for signs of tampering is an important aspect of your personal security program.* To perform such a search, you must first familiarize yourself with your car, and especially its undercarriage and engine area.

The search starts with a walk around the car before entering. Be sure the doors are still locked and the windows are completely closed. Look for suspicious grease smudges, dirt streaks and tool marks near windows, doors, hood and trunk lid.

Now move down to the undercarriage and check for objects near the tires and in the tailpipe, unfamiliar or new wires around the engine area, and newly cleaned spots.

If everything looks normal, open the car door and look under the dash for foreign objects and unusual hanging wires. Remember, you are not looking for a bomb. You are looking for *signs* of a bomb.

---

*If you are a known potential target of any non-criminal threat group or if you live in an area where car bombings are not uncommon: beware! If you detect any signs of tampering call the police immediately. Do not attempt to enter, start, or drive your car. Do not attempt to find the bomb itself. Leave the area immediately.

A final word of advice about car searches: trust your instincts. If something just does not look right, it probably isn't.

PARKING SECURITY

The last consideration about car security is certainly the most important. It is the everyday routine you use in order to keep your car secure, and avoid excessive anxiety about markings, bombs, break-ins, or thefts. Contrary to what may seem logical, it is easier to keep your car secure in most areas overseas than it is in the United States. The reason for this is simple. Cars generally cost much more, insurance is very costly, and guards or lot attendants are often cheap. Thus people find it more important to keep their car secure.

You and every driver in your family must learn to take a number of basic precautions when parking your vehicle. Always park in a secure or guarded garage whenever possible, and never leave your keys with a parking attendant. If you must park in an unguarded area, do so in the busiest, most visible location possible. Be sure all car doors are locked and the windows rolled up tight before leaving the parking area.

Should conditions demand that you leave your car on an unlit side street in the middle of the night in a bad section of town, leave your car at home and take a cab!

Defensive Driving

Defensive driving is the combination of techniques used by the individual driver while in his car to detect, avoid, and if necessary, counter, potential attacks by violent elements. Most of you probably have some knowledge of defensive driving due to its recent coverage by the media. The large number of recent sensational attacks by terrorists on important people has stirred the media to produce a plethora of information on defensive driving and the schools and people that teach it. Unfortunately for everyone concerned, much of the media's attention has been concentrated on the driver's ability to handle his car in the actual attack situation. In fact, your ability to practice safe driving methods and detect surveillance is of far greater importance than is your ability to ram through a roadblock or perform a perfect bootleg turn. Actually, it is very easy to both learn safe driving methods, and surveillance detection, while the skills required to drive in an attack situation can be quite difficult to develop.

So what I will teach you primarily is how to *avoid* an attack situation while in your car. I will also cover the basic driving manuevers used during an attack situation, but only to the extent that you can reasonably expect to gain by it. For the vast majority of Americans, this will be more than sufficient to provide a level of security commensurate to the likely threat. For those who feel a need for more training, I recommend that you take a defensive driving course, as offered by several schools around the country. What these schools offer that cannot be found in this book is hands-on driving practice in the attack situation. Do not expect to learn any great secrets or become a "James Bond style driver" by attending a defensive driving school. What they can and do teach you is what a car can really do if required, versus what you thought it could do; how to recognize most common attack situations; how to actually drive in an attack situation; and how to be confident in your new skills.

The great problem with defensive driving in the attack scenario is that no one can teach you how to recognize every possible attack situation, which defensive or offensive technique is called for, and how to make sure you will react properly when the situation actually occurs. The possible variables in the attack situation are many. Careful study of the appropriate part of this chapter and attendance at a defensive driving school are both important, but put your emphasis on doing those things which will help you avoid an attack altogether. That is where you have the most control and where you can do yourself the most good.

Defensive Driving Techniques

There are three primary areas of defensive driving techniques: avoidance, detection, and countering the attack. *Avoidance* entails the methods you employ in order to avoid becoming a target in the first place. *Detection* involves the recognition of surveillance and hence the knowledge that you have become a potential target and may soon be attacked. *Countering the attack* involves the methods you employ in both recognizing that an attack is about to begin or has begun, and the manner in which you must handle it to escape.

Avoidance

Avoidance is the simplest and yet most important of the three areas of defensive driving. It only requires a little planning and effort on your part, and strict adherence to some basic defensive driving techniques.

As stated before, after a terrorist or criminal group has chosen you as a potential target, they will assess your possible value to them, and try to determine the weakest link in your personal security program. Assuming you have adequately protected yourself in other areas, the terrorist will likely check your car security. This may be done by acquiring intelligence on you from somebody who has knowledge of your patterns, or by actually surveilling you for at least a few days. If your avoidance techniques are good, he may well decide that the amount of work required to successfully attack you in your car is outweighed by your limited value in terms of kidnapping or assassination. Why should he waste so much of his time and effort to attack you, when other targets of equal value will present much less trouble? This is not only common sense but human nature, and it is exactly what you are trying to accomplish.

AVOIDANCE GUIDELINES

Basically, the intent of your avoidance measures is to refrain from driving in any areas where you and your auto could be easily targetted. That is why I call avoidance the simplest of the three areas encompassed in defensive driving: all you have to do is avoid driving in dangerous-looking situations.

Yet it may be difficult to detect hazardous situations every moment you are driving. For this reason you must always obey the basic safety car principles, such as buckling your seat belt, rolling up your windows, and so on. You must always be prepared to take evasive, drastic actions, even though this is what you are intentionally trying to avoid.

I also include route and routine variation under the avoidance category. I have stressed its importance before, and will do so again. You must consistently vary every routine that is a part of your daily schedule. Unpredictability and variation clearly will allow you to avoid potential trackers. So vary your driving routes any time you leave your home or office, whether to and from work, errancs, or entertainment. Try to avoid becoming a regular patron of any one club, restaurant, or shop.

Remember to inform your family, friends, or associates of your planned unpredictability. Someone trustworthy should be updated on trip plans just in case you fail to arrive on time. Use your in-car radio to report any delays, schedule or destination changes. Drive with two or more people whenever possible.

Another diversionary tactic is a car-switching pool, rotating vehicles on a random basis with a friend or associate. Two-car families should switch cars unpredictably every few days. Occasionally take a taxi, bus, train, or ride with a friend to vary both route and routine.

Pay special attention to the logistics to and from your home and office, as most car attacks occur close to the point of departure or destination. Change—*often*—the ways you get there and back.

In planning trips of any distance, try to use highways and regularly traveled roads with a minimum number of stops. Wide roads are safer than narrow, winding ones, and you should drive as close to the center of the road as possible. Drive by police stations or military barracks rather than through the seedy side of town. Alleys, side streets, and one-way single lane roads must be circumvented, as well as tunnels, bridges, and overpasses in lightly traveled areas. Temporary detours, backroads, and unusual shortcuts detract from driving security.

Detecting Surveillance

Detecting surveillance is the primary means you have at your disposal to help find out if you have become the potential target of some threat element and may soon face an attack situation. However, the fact that you are being surveilled does not necessarily mean that you will ultimately be attacked. If your personal security program is well planned and well performed, it may simply mean that the surveillant will decide your security is very good and that an attack might be very difficult, and is not worth the effort. But you should always take surveillance seriously. If and when you detect surveillance, report it immediately to the police and to the U.S. Embassy. Give them as much information about the surveillance as possible. Increase your security to the degree possible and eliminate all unnecessary trips away from your home or office. If possible, take a vacation out of the country. Watch for any continued surveillance and have your friends and family help you.

Surveillance is not always undertaken just by terrorists. It is possible you will find that the surveillant is planning to either rob you, steal your car, or burglarize your house. He may even be a member of the local police or security service. The local police and security services often become interested in American businessmen whom they suspect may be involved in black marketing, bribery, payoffs, or espionage. Do not underestimate the number of non-western governments that believe every American businessman or government official living abroad works for the CIA. It is simply mind boggling.

Detecting surveillance can be a difficult process but this is not generally the case. Good surveillance teams are generally limited to a small number of governments and a select group of terrorist organizations. Even these surveillance teams will make mistakes or perform actions that make them detectable by their target.

Detecting surveillance is largely a matter of knowing what to look for, keeping your eyes open, and not believing in coincidence. For example, if a blue Fiat with a broken windshield follows you somewhere two days in a row, it is possibly a coincidence. If it follows you somewhere again, two days later, it is probably surveillance. If it follows you anywhere within the following few days, it *is* surveillance.

Surveillance will generally start at your house and continue to your destination. It will generally cover your entire day's routine up to the end. It may take a variety of forms but will generally include surveillance by another automobile, van, truck, or other vehicle. Practice all of the following guidelines carefully. If you think you have spotted surveillance, make complete notes as to type, description, time, place, and persons. Do not do anything to let the surveillants know they have been detected. If the surveillance continues, notify the proper authorities and give them all the information you have. Follow their instructions but look out for your interests.

SURVEILLANCE DETECTION GUIDELINES

Keep a discreet eye peeled for anyone, pedestrians or people in parked vehicles, watching as you enter your car. Since moving surveillance usually begins immediately after you pull away, note anyone following during the first few blocks.

Be a mirror watcher as you drive and stay aware of any car that pulls out of a parking place, side street, or driveway, and appears to trail you. But remember surveillants will not necessarily tailgate, so look for the car staying several cars or half a block behind. Or they may track from the front, side, or another street.

Learn to memorize license plates or car makes at a glance, enough so the number or model is familiar if you encounter it continually. Remembering each and every car is not necessary or practical, but if a real pattern develops, the information may prove critical.

Surveillance vehicles are often as nondescript as your anti-surveillance vehicle. Any surveillant worth his salt will switch cars within the course of one trip or from day to day. Look for surveillance vehicles with younger drivers, for there are very few old terrorists.

Do not expect surveillants to hound you to your doorstep. Once sure of your destination and route, the surveillance team probably will break off and set up to follow you again when you leave.

If you suspect you really *are* under surveillance, double check your theory with someone else. Have a friend follow you discreetly, or drive by your friend's house, so he can watch to see if you are being tracked. Never "play" with surveillants, such as making U-turns, running red lights, or speeding unless you are truly in an emergency situation or believe an attack is imminent.

Countering the Attack

Hopefully, if you have worked hard at avoidance and detection, you will not have to face the problem of countering an attack. However, the possibility always exists that your best efforts will have been in vain and that a violent attack will occur. You must be prepared to meet this challenge, counter it, and survive. There are no hard and fast rules on how to counter and escape from any particular attack that may take place while you are in your car. It is a case of "not how you play the game, but whether you win or lose." There are some general guidelines that you should follow and some specific things you can look for and do in the event of an attack.

There are five factors that seem always to play crucial parts in those situations where an American overseas has survived a vehicular attack and escaped:

1. The individual had a good knowledge of the threat situation in his area and how that might affect him.
2. The individual had at least a basic understanding of personal security, including elements of defensive driving, and took care to apply what he knew.
3. The individual had a strong will to survive and escape any attack.
4. The individual was decisive when the attack was recognized.
5. The individual intentionally tried to escape.

Everyone who reads this book and applies its principles should have no trouble accomplishing the first two points. The third point is up to you, the individual. But make the decision now. Do not wait until an attack takes place. Naturally, there may be a situation where escape is impossible. But what will you do if it seems a good risk? Carefully consider the situation in your area. If an attack is likely to mean an assassination attempt, then by all means you should try to escape at any cost. But if an attack will probably result in a kidnapping for a low ransom and certain release, than an escape might only be contemplated when the odds are well in your favor. Think about it. Talk about it. Consider it carefully now. There will be precious little time, if any, once an attack has begun.

The fourth point, decisiveness, is of paramount importance. Once you have recognized an attack, you must quickly decide your immediate actions. You will probably only have a matter of seconds and they will be crucial to your success. If you do not make a decision quickly and take appropriate action, it will be made for you by the speed of events. And remember the old saying: "A bad decision well executed is better than no decision at all."

The fifth point is perhaps the simplest. Once you have decided to try to escape, do so. Do not wait for a mistake on the part of the attackers, a moment to see what develops, or a *deus ex machina* to save you. No one is going to help you. You have to do it alone. Hope is for those who cannot help themselves and it is a luxury you will not be able to afford. Once you have decided to escape, make your plan, and follow it through.

Handling an Attack

Now let's consider the four major elements relevant to handling a car attack. They are: *added security measures, attack recognition and evaluation, countermeasures and escape,* and *post attack actions.*

ADDED AUTO SECURITY MEASURES

Included in this category are professional drivers, vehicular bodyguards, armored cars, and escort vehicles.

A professional driver can be a worthwhile investment if you live in a high threat environment where vehicular attacks are common. However, for the money, I suggest always choosing an armored car over a driver, or even vehicular bodyguards. The armored car offers the best protection for the investment (see next chapter for armored car purchase details).

Should you choose to hire a driver, he must be professionally trained in defensive driving, and capable of decisive, positive action in the event of an attack. The driver may also be a trained bodyguard. This is ideal. Both driver and vehicular bodyguard must be willing to protect you with their lives, for they may well have to. (See next chapter for complete details on hiring, instructing and personal treatment of bodyguards in general).

If you can afford it, hire two or more vehicular bodyguards.

Escort vehicles should only be considered if you already have an armored car. They represent a substantial expense, since they should have all the high performance and security modifications I recommend for your own car. They must also be manned by guards and drivers who are professionally trained, and armed.

ATTACK RECOGNITION AND EVALUATION

The primary rule to remember in recognizing an attack situation is to always view the unusual or peculiar as a potential danger. Recognizing an attack may be extremely difficult. Anything that happens while you drive, that is not an everyday occurrence, should be viewed as a potential attack situation. When such an event takes place, consider it carefully, and be prepared to act. Naturally, some attacks will be blatant. In these cases you will have to act instantly.

Consider the following scenarios. Any one of them may indicate an impending attack, or depending on the time span, an attack in progress. Some situations may prove harmless, while others may prove deadly.

- A pedestrian jumping in front of your car.
- A bicyclist falling in front of your car.
- A baby carriage pushed in front of your car.
- A "heart attack" victim falling in front of your car.
- A flagman stopping your car.
- Workmen blocking your car.
- Survey personnel stopping your car.
- A faked police, military, or government checkpoint or blockade.
- A disabled vehicle blocking the road.
- The "victim of an accident" flagging you down for assistance.

- A truck unloading farm equipment, or fallen tree blocking the street.
- An unusual street detour sign.
- An accident in which your car is negligently struck by another.
- Cars to your front and/or back, or pulling in from the side, slowing down, and blocking you.
- Simultaneous approach by several people while your car is stopped due to traffic or a blocking vehicle.
- Simultaneous flattening or blowouts of more than one tire.
- Sudden and extreme commotion, movement, or gunfire near your car.

It is obvious from the above that recognizing a developing attack may be difficult. Certainly these signs are obvious, but can you be sure? The answer is no. In a few instances, such as a roadblock, there will be little or no doubt in your mind. But even if someone is trying to run you off the road it may be difficult to determine his exact intentions.

The answer to all of this is fairly simple. If any of these situations occur you should try to escape the area immediately. If you can do so without taking another's life, then you have nothing to lose. It may cost you some money for property damage but that should not be your concern. If escape means taking someone's life by hitting him with your car, then you must judge the situation quickly and make the most difficult decision on your own.

If you are being intentionally forced off the road, you have every right to ram your way out, even if it may cause the other party injury or death. But if you simply see several people approaching your car, can you afford to run over them without the certain knowledge that they intend to kidnap or kill you? There is no sure, general answer. Only time will teach what is normal behavior in your particular location. You will quickly learn to judge for yourself what is simply an unusual occurrence and what may be a trap. If the situation *demands* you wait before making a decision, then do so, but only if a safe and nonprovocative escape cannot be made. If any of these situations represent a trap, you will know it shortly. Hostile movements, extreme and violent commotions, and shots will certainly settle any of your doubts. But even in this prolonged situation you may still have time for escape. Your options are open until you are out of your car and someone has a gun to your head.

COUNTERMEASURES AND ESCAPE

Once you recognize that an attack has begun you have two options. You can either accept the situation and be harmed, assassinated, or kidnapped—or you can try to escape. If you choose to escape there are essentially two modes of action you can take: offensive and defensive. *Defensive action* is characterized by removing yourself from the scene of the attack without directly engaging your attacker. *Offensive action* is characterized by an escape that requires a sudden and violent action against your attacker in order to break free of his trap. Which type action you choose will depend upon the circumstances and upon your individual propensities.

Before we consider these actions and how they are applied, return for a moment to the subject of your car. If you have purchased a car in accordance with the recommendations in this chapter, you will have several distinct advantages. The car's engine will have extra power. The car will have good handling characteristics, and a substantial ramming capability. You will also have at your disposal a siren or foghorn. These options will give you added abilities in countering an attack. They will help you to do some things you might not expect. First, your car will be able to ram out of virtually any kind of blocking situation. Aimed at the right place, a VW bug can knock a Cadillac out of its way. Second, your engine will have the brute force needed to push any car you ram, and literally move it out of the way if necessary. Third, your steering, brakes, and suspension will give you the ability to handle your car in a violent manner yet still maintain control. Fourth, your siren, which should be turned on as soon as an attack is recognized, will both surprise the attacker and draw the attention of anyone nearby, especially the police.

Knowing what these options give you is not enough. You must understand what your car is capable of. It can sustain serious damage and still run. It can still go even if all four tires are shot out. It can jump curbs, ram through fences, knock down small trees, drive through farmers' fields, sustain multiple bullet holes, and still carry you safely away. Above all, it can be a deadly weapon. You must learn that your car is a machine with the capability of doing things for which it was not designed. You have been conditioned by driving experience back in the States, and also by the traffic laws that restrict its use there. But when overseas, you need to forget your old conditioning and traffic laws. If attacked, you will have every right to ram other cars, drive on sidewalks, go the wrong way down one-way streets, and use other measures of this kind. So do not be limited by habit in an emergency. Use your car in whatever way necessary to help you escape. Do not be afraid. Your car can take a severe beating, dish one out, and still save your life.

Now let's look at some car attack situations:

Situation #1. You have recognized an attack situation at least 100 meters ahead of you. Your immediate response is defensive. Check to see you have not been blocked in from behind. If you are a trained defensive driver you might execute a J-turn or bootleg turn. If you are not, then make an immediate U-turn. Use the sidewalk or other area adjacent to the street if necessary but avoid having to stop and back up to complete the turn. If necessary, put the car in reverse, back up as quickly and as far as possible, and then execute a U-turn, or turn off on to a side street. Proceed away from the scene as fast as possible and seek help. Unless you are in a remote area the chances are you will not be followed.

Situation #2. You are on a narrow street and the road ahead of you is blocked by one or two cars turned sideways across the road. You check behind you and see that you have been blocked from the rear. You realize that it is an attack situation and you choose to try to escape. Continue driving toward the blockade as if you are not sure what is happening. Slow down a bit, then drop your car into low gear. Now step on the gas! If you are being blocked by a single car, attempt to strike it with your outside bumper just above its rear wheel well. If you are being blocked by two cars you may try the same ram so long as you have room to get around that particular car. In general though, you should attempt to strike both cars where they meet in the center of the street. Keep your foot on the accelerator. Don't let it off until you are clear of the area.

You may also wish to time your ram in a different manner. If your attackers are still in their blocking cars, wait until they open the doors and start to step out. Time your ram to coincide with their attempted exist. This will not only defeat their blockade but disable them and keep them from shooting at you while you escape.

Situation #3. You are traveling down a narrow road. A car appears to be passing you when suddenly he swerves in front of you and attempts to run you off the road or stop you. Just as his car turns in front of you, turn your car into his car and hit the side nearest you, at the rear wheel well or behind, with the end of your front bumper which is nearest his car. Accelerate your engine. As his car begins to turn sideways, straighten your car out and drive right through him. His car will easily be pushed out of the way. Drive away quickly.

Situation #4. You are driving down the road and a car begins to slow down in front of you. You see to the left that another car is directly beside you and blocking you in. Both cars begin to brake fast and you realize an attack has begun. Brake only enough to avoid heavily ramming the car in front of you. Hit your accelerator. Turn sharply to the left so that your left front bumper hits the front wheel well of the car to your side. You will simultaneously strike the left rear bumper of the car to your front. Keep your wheel turned and continue accelerating. You will push both cars out of the way. When you have broken free of the blocking attempt get away as fast as possible and seek help.

Situation #5. You are driving in light traffic. The car in front of you has suddenly and heavily braked. You make an emergency stop and perhaps even strike the rear of the car to your front. Suddenly you are hit from behind. Probably an unfortunate accident. But quickly you note that someone in the car in front of you has jumped out with a gun. An irate motorist? Perhaps, but it does not really matter. Someone is still trying to do you bodily harm. You immediately hit the accelerator. Pushing the car ahead of you, you turn slightly in the direction of the man with the gun. In this manner you are moving the car out of the way, putting yourself in a position to go around it, and at the same time forcing the gunman to quickly move out of the way. or face being run over. Once around the car you duck down and speed away.

Situation #6. You are driving alone on a remote country road when you come upon a one-lane bridge. As you start to cross the bridge a bulldozer pulls up on the other side blocking your way. You look behind you and see that a tractor trailer has pulled up behind you. Suddenly you notice upwards of fifty heavily armed men rushing at you from both your front and back. You look down from the bridge and see a drop of 150 feet onto jagged rocks. What do you do? Put your car in park, turn the ignition off, light up a cigarette, and relax. Maybe you can convince them it's a case of mistaken identity. In any case, you cannot win them all.

Moral: know when you are licked. If the situation should ever parallel the last one described, do not try to escape. The chances are you would be killed, or at best, injured. If you are inevitably going to be captured, your survival chances are far better if you are uninjured and have not injured or killed any of your attackers.

The first five situations illustrate several important points to remember if you find yourself involved in a vehicular attack. Basically, if you can manage a getaway, do it. Turn away, make a U-turn, drive over medians, sidewalks, or lawns to skip the scene entirely.

When there is no chance to escape without direct confrontation, assume the offensive. Remember your car is ready to ram. Aim your car at a point from the front wheel well forward or the rear wheel well back and hit the other car at an angle. Always accelerate as you strike and continue accelerating through the ram until you have broken free.

POST ATTACK ACTIONS

After making your escape and reaching a place of protection, report the attack in detail to local authorities and the U.S. embassy. Analyze why you were a target and whether that status will persist. If the attack was a kidnapping effort, your escape may be answered by an attempt to kill you. Depending on the particular circumstances, decide either to upgrade your security or immediately leave the country.

11
BOTTOM LINE
SECURITY

It is appropriate at this point to look at some bottom line security measures you may want to consider to help you improve your personnel security while living abroad. For some of you these options may appear to be inappropriate or simply not cost-effective. Depending on your particular situation you may be right. Note that the options discussed in this chapter are limited to those that offer realistic answers to increased personal security needs and are generally considered the most effective in the overseas environment.

The options to be discussed are: lethal and non-lethal weapons, body armor and portable antiballistic devices, armored cars, guards, bodyguards, and civilian security services. For most of you the sections on weapons and guards will have some relevance because these are commonly exercised options for people living in a threat environment. For those of you who may face a high risk situation, consider the other options carefully. They may be relevant to your needs.

Lethal and Non-lethal Weapons

For many of you the idea of owning a gun, much less ever using one, may seem abhorrent. It is not my intention to dispel any such belief but only to provide you with some basic and necessary information, should you opt for a gun on your overseas assignment. Furthermore, there are certain non-lethal weapons which may be appropriate to those who prefer such devices.

Lethal Weapons

Among lethal weapons, the firearm is the most conspicuous and widely used for the purpose of self-defense. Before going on an overseas assignment, you need to consider four areas concerning gun ownership; *Legal Aspects, The Question of Necessity, Preparedness,* and *When the Need Arises.*

LEGAL ASPECTS

Gun laws vary drastically from country to country and you should check these out before trying to take a gun into the country of your assignment. This is best done by contacting the particular country's embassy in your present location. They will be able to tell you what the laws are, what is required, and how to go about getting a gun into the country, if it is legal. You should also ascertain the safest manner in which your gun can be brought into the country. In some countries if it arrives with your air freight, marked and listed for customs inspection, you may never see it again. If it shows up in your bags at the airport, you may spend a long afternoon explaining to the police why you brought it with you. So be thorough and make sure your gun will both arrive and be legal.

Ammunition is another consideration. Some countries will let you bring in a gun but no ammunition. Only a few shippers will handle ammunition and it is an involved process. The best solution is to make sure you purchase a gun for which ammunition can be purchased locally. It may not be top quality ammunition but it will usually suffice.

But what if you think you need a gun and they are not allowed? The answer to this question is largely a matter of weighing the need against the possible penalty. If the need is great and the penalty is small, then it may be worth having an "illegal" gun. The best solution to this problem is to wait until you arrive at your location and see what the situation really is. What you may have heard from the embassy or other sources may have little to do with the realities that exist. If guns are illegal but everybody has one, then you will not find it difficult to purchase one yourself. In many foreign countries there are laws against handguns but they often apply, in reality, only to the poor. Once you are in-country you will be able to better judge your needs and take action as appropriate. But do not fight city hall. If handguns are illegal but shotguns are not, then by all means just take your shotgun. It will serve the purpose of self-defense very well.

THE QUESTION OF NECESSITY

The matter of whether a gun is necessary for your self-defense is something only you can decide. If you normally keep a gun in your home in the States, then you will probably be uncomfortable if you do not have one overseas. But if you do not normally keep a gun at home, then this becomes a more important decision. Your decision should then be based on probable need. Carefully go over your threat analysis. What is your threat profile? Will owning a gun actually enhance your security? These are just a couple of the questions you will have to answer for yourself. There is only one thing I would add. Do not dismiss a gun outright. A different world lies beyond those oceans, and in at least a few of the more remote areas owning a gun is not simply an option but a basic tool of survival.

PREPAREDNESS

There is little point in owning a gun if you do not know how to use it. So if you have a gun make sure you know how it works, how to take care of it, and how to hit what you are aiming at. A gun in the hand of a novice is an accident waiting to happen. If you are a novice and planning to own a gun, do some homework. Get someone experienced with firearms to help you. And make sure you practice what you learn.

WHEN THE NEED ARISES

Whether or not you will be able to use a gun if the need arises is really up to you, and you alone. No one can answer this question until he has experienced a situation that calls for the use of a gun. The point to remember here is that you will not know until you have tried. Therefore, do not dismiss the idea of taking a gun along simply because you think you will not have the nerve to use it. That decision is best left until your particular moment of reckoning.

Choice of Firearms
Let's look at the various types of guns and how they may serve you in the self-defense role:

RIFLES

Rifles are generally not a very effective weapon for the purpose of self-defense around the house. However, they do have their place. If you live in an environment of civil war or revolution and in a more remote area, you may find a rifle to be a useful weapon. It is essentially a weapon for open combat rather than self-defense.

SHOTGUNS

These are excellent self-defense weapons as they are usually both legal and effective. They provide easy operation, adequate range, and excellent firepower. They are fairly safe to keep around the house, and can be effectively used by just about anybody. The gauge is not so important as the mode and ammunition you use. Avoid an over-and-under or a side-by-side double barrel. Choose a five-shot repeating model and make sure the magazine is not blocked. Keep a box of double 0/0 buckshot to use for your self-defense ammunition.

HANDGUNS

With few exceptions, the handgun's primary role is for shooting people. The problem is that it seldom winds up being used by the right people, at the right time, and for the right purpose. If you decide to choose a handgun, make sure you know how to use it. Keep it safely out of reach of the kids yet in an accessible place. A handgun will not be of much use if it is locked in your safe at the critical moment.

The best handgun for the lesser experienced person is probably a .38 caliber revolver. It is simple to use, packs sufficient power, and works almost every time. For those who will face a serious threat, know how to handle a gun, and feel they may have to use one, the 9mm automatic with double action is probably the best selection. It offers speed, power, and a large clip of ammunition.

Whatever handgun you choose, make sure it meets the following requirements:

- At least a .38 caliber.
- High quality and reputable brand name.
- Double action.
- Safety.
- Easy to operate.
- Comfortable to your grip.
- Reliable functioning.

The other lethal weapons which you might wish to consider are knives, hatchets, machetes, or other bladed instruments. Forget about these weapons! Unless you have had extensive military, police, or professional training, you are likely to gain no advantage by brandishing an edged weapon. In fact, you are likely to aggravate an already bad situation and probably get yourself killed. Knives may be useful to muggers and rapists but have at best a questionable self-defense role for you.

In summation, the lethal weapons have their place in self-defense and personal security if they are handled and used properly. The most important thing to remember about lethal weapons is that they are LETHAL. Never carry a gun unless you absolutely must. Never keep a gun at home unless you know how to use it. Never pick up a gun unless you are prepared to use it. Never aim it at anyone unless you intend to shoot at him. Never shoot at someone unless you intend to kill him. And never kill anyone unless you are sure of who it is, why you are doing it, and that there is no other choice.

Non-lethal Weapons

Non-lethal weapons have a limited usefulness against the various violent elements you may face overseas. Their attraction is that they may offer you some element of surprise and a degree of distraction. Their fault is that they do not offer sufficient protection, and like knives, may only aggravate the situation.

Chemical sprays and gases are a common form of non-lethal weapons used by many women and some men. They are generally effective only if aimed directly into an assailant's face, and even then will not necessarily stop a determined foe. They are good for use against muggers and rapists if they are the only available weapon, but will be of little value against terrorists. A device which may be more useful in both situations is the pocket size emergency airhorn. There are many of these on the market and most are effective. They can be easily activated, will make a very loud noise, will continue to operate automatically for several minutes, and are almost impossible to turn off.

Another group of non-lethal weapons includes clubs. Whether it is a policeman's nightstick, a pipe, bat, or wrench is not of any great importance. It is a basic weapon that can be used in a close quarter struggle to give you a distinct advantage in hand-to-hand combat. It is useful against burglars, vandals, and similar types but offers no protection against *anyone* with a gun, much less an armed terrorist.

While there are many other types of non-lethal weapons, almost none will offer any worthwhile advantage. There is one weapon exception, however, that may be worth considering. It is a weapon that offers the advantages of deadly force without the lethal consequences. It is the electric gun, more commonly known as the Taser. The Taser is a hand held squarish looking device that resembles a large flashlight with a handle grip. Battery powered, the Taser shoots a pair of small barbed darts that embed in the clothing of the victim. Electricity passes instantly through two thin wires between the gun and the darts, and the victim is immediately "immobilized" by the electrical charge.

The intent of the Taser's inventor was to produce a weapon for self-defense which would have the same effect as a deadly shot from a gun, but without actually damaging the victim. In principle, the gun works perfectly, its only drawback being its limited range (about six feet) and, naturally, the need for the shooter to aim well enough to hit the victim. Unfortunately, the weapon cannot just be used for self-defense but also for violent crime.

For the purpose of self-defense and personal security abroad the Taser may have a place. It is a viable alternative to the handgun. It will probably not be of much use against a concerted attack by a violent group but can be of value against a burglar, thief, or single assailant. If you wish to investigate this weapon further, contact your local gun store.*

Body Armor

The recent advances in body armor technology make it a worthwhile consideration for anyone facing a serious threat situation. Body armor can provide you with a last line of defense that can save your life in an attack situation. Modern body armor is primarily made of Kevlar (the only kind you should buy) and is lightweight, cheap, relatively comfortable, and generally effective. Additionally, it can be easily disguised under jackets, sportcoats, or overcoats, so that it is difficult for anyone to notice you are wearing it. Perhaps the most important aspect of modern armor is that it not only works, but can be worn with relative comfort. The comfort factor has always been one of the great inhibitors to people who have felt a need to wear body armor. The result in the past has been that owners of body armor simply left it at home. That is no longer a problem and should not deter you from using it now if you have the need. Body armor can be purchased in standard clothing sizes or custom fitted to tailored precision.

Body armor in disguised form is of considerable value because most of us are a little embarrassed about wearing it (which we should not be), and because we can keep the knowledge of wearing it from the potential attacker. The importance of keeping your attacker ignorant of your armor is simply to keep him from shooting you in an area of the body which is not protected; e.g., your head. It may also give you the option of "playing dead" should the situation warrant it.

Besides this disguised body armor there is also the regular version which can be purchased to be worn over your clothes or under them. Most of this type armor takes the form of the vest or T-shirt type but may include a full body covering. In addi-

---

*The Taser is illegal in some states and foreign countries. Check the local laws carefully before taking one with you to your overseas destination.

tion there are "area protectors" which are designed to protect specific parts of the body such as knees or the groin area.

When purchasing body armor it is more important to judge what it does, how it looks, and how it feels, than it is to concern yourself with how it actually works. Just be sure the vest is made of Kevlar.

Another point to remember when considering the purchase of body armor is that it is not something that has to be worn twenty-four hours a day. In general, you should not need to wear it while at home or in the office. It is essentially an item that is limited to use when you are in a public situation. It should be worn when driving, walking, eating out and in similar situations. Thus, even if you find it slightly cumbersome, you will only have to wear it part of the time.

If you wish to investigate body armor further, contact your local police equipment supply store or a manufacturer.

Portable Antiballistic Devices

Portable antiballistic devices represent virtually any device that can be hand carried and used as a shield to stop bullets. The most common of these, and the one I will discuss, is the armored briefcase. The armored briefcase is simply a standard briefcase with a piece of lightweight armored plating mounted on one of its inside walls. Its primary purpose is to be used like a shield. In an attack situation it can be held in front of the chest to give you protection similar to that of an armored vest. It is essentially a panic tool and will only afford you a limited amount of protection since your attacker may quickly choose to shoot at another open part of your body. Yet I know of at least one incident when an armored briefcase saved its owner's life in the manner just described. The attacker fired several times into the briefcase and when nothing happened, ran away.

The armored briefcase is a worthwhile asset. It will provide you at least some degree of protection and that may be a lot, depending on the situation. It is cheap, well disguised, not much heavier than a normal briefcase, and will stop bullets or a knife. You can make one yourself by simply buying a cut piece of lightweight armor and gluing it to the inner wall of your briefcase, or it may be purchased outright from police equipment supply stores.

Armored Cars

The armored car is an important tool in the field of personal security for those who have a genuine need. An armored car can be either partially or fully armored and—depending upon the quality, completeness, and level of protection provided—can be a substantial aid for defense against vehicular attack.

The primary question is whether you will need one. For the vast majority the answer is "no." For some the answer is "maybe," and for a few the answer is "yes." How to determine which answer is appropriate to you is simply a matter of determining your realistic need. The questions to consider are: How high is the threat level in my location? How common are vehicular attacks in my location? What is my own threat profile?

Realistically speaking, only those Americans who will live in an area of intense terrorist activity, where vehicular attacks are fairly common, and who have a high threat profile, should consider having an armored car at their disposal. Most Americans should find that a good defensive driving program will satisfactorily suit their needs in this area. In addition to being an unnecessary expense, owning an armored car in an area where you do not need one may only attract a lot of unwanted attention.

There are a number of considerations to review if an armored car is a necessary part of your security program. The cost, for one, often proves prohibitive for private individuals, as $20,000 is the starting price for an armored car with fully protected cabin. This major investment deserves major attention from you, your employer (especially if he foots the bill), and the seller. A professional consultant can save money, time, and trouble.

Observe standard operating procedure for any primary purchase: shop around, avoid hard sells, and get guarantees. In particular for assessing armored cars, remember that fancy gizmos require fancy drivers. Buy only what you need. Look for a company that will furnish a defensive driving course with the car.

Test drive the car to make sure it handles well in both normal and emergency driving conditions, not on the seller's parking lot, but on wet, rough, hilly, winding, dark roads. Settle the insurance and shipping arrangements to your overseas location before leaving home.

WHAT TO LOOK FOR

First you must decide whether you want a fully or partially armored car. A fully armored car is normally recognized as one which affords the passenger compartment general all-around protection from attack by certain weapons and ammunitions. However, that does not necessarily mean the car is armored in either the roof or floor. Nor does it mean there are not very small gaps between the armoring in certain areas, or that bolts are protected. Verify these points with the manufacturer and consider them according to your needs.

A partially armored car is one in which certain areas of the car have been armored to provide protection from specific types of weapons and ammunition. In general, partial armoring is applied to the doors, firewall, and rear trunk wall to provide the passenger compartment a degree of protection from armed assault. While many manufacturers tend to dismiss partial armoring as ineffective, I disagree. Full armoring is no doubt the most desirable solution, but some armoring is better than none. This is especially true if you genuinely need an armored car but for whatever reason cannot afford one. This is no small matter when you consider that a car can be partially armored (doors, firewall, rear trunk) for as little as $2500. A fully armored car begins at almost ten times that amount.

The disadvantages of a partially armored car versus a fully armored car are obvious. Suffice it to say that a partially armored car offers you one distinct advantage over a car with no armoring: it gives you the option to try to escape an attack when you might otherwise not even consider it.

Partially armored cars should meet the armoring specifications you want plus all the requirements and options as discussed in chapter 10. Fully armored cars should meet these same requirements, plus have all the equipment and options listed below:

- No luxury or sports cars. Cadillacs and Mercedes are definitely out unless you have no reason or desire to keep a low profile.
- High performance engine capable of powering the car in a manner similar to that of the same make and model car without armoring.
- Heavy-duty automatic transmission.
- Automatic locks for doors.
- Four-door model.
- Reinforced chassis, suspension, and brakes.
- Secure message and communication port for driver's door.
- Non-exploding or crashworthy, self-sealing fuel tank.
- No-flat tires.
- Reinforced front wheel wells.
- Armoring to fit your needs and requirements.

ARMOR SELECTION
The armoring itself is the guts of any "bulletproof" car and you will find a lot of diversity in the industry. I cannot give you any universal guidance on armoring, and this is why you should get some help or do a lot of homework and shopping around. Basically, any "fully armored" car should provide all-around protection to the entire passenger/driver area. Some people choose not to armor the roof simply because it is not a common area of attack. If I could afford it I would probably armor the roof but only with lightweight armor. The same goes for the floor. My reasoning here is that bullets ricochet off pavement and it is possible that a stray round could enter through the floor. Whatever you do, do not armor the floor to withstand any bomb blast. It is simply not worth it since most bombs planted under cars have enough explosive power to blow the car to pieces anyway.

The armor itself comes in different types, weights, and thicknesses in order to meet your ballistic requirements. Your ballistic requirements simply define what type of weapon, round, and bullet velocity you wish the car to be able to withstand. It is very important that you only establish a ballistic requirement that is consistent with the weapons used by the violent elements in your area. The heavier your requirements, the heavier and more expensive the car. In any case, you should try to buy a car with as much lightweight armor as possible. While heavy steel plate armor is just as good and can provide the same ballistic protection, it is substantially heavier and can affect the overall performance of the car. This is no small point when trying to stop on a wet cobblestone road.

If you know nothing of the type of weapons you will face, ask the manufacturer to provide you with a car that meets Underwriters Laboratories' Ballistic Level III. This level of armoring will protect you against most of the common small arms used by criminals and terrorists around the world. Anything less than this might be taking a chance and anything more will add a lot of weight to the car. While some manufacturers do not like to talk about any UL ballistic level, it is at least a place to start.

All window areas should be armored with multi-shot capacity transparent armor. Transparent armor is what will appear to be very thick "glass." Multi-shot capacity means that it will absorb several bullets within inches of each other and still hold up.

You should also make sure that there is no space between sections of armor. The good manufacturer will ensure that cracks and gaps are eliminated by either overlapping the armor or backing it up with additional armor sections. It is also important to make sure that all bolts and hard points are designed to withstand bullet impact. If not they can become lethal shrapnel inside your car.

The key to getting good armor is the same as getting the right car. Go to a reputable dealer. His very survival as a business is dependent upon your survival while in your car.

To locate a reputable armored car manufacturer, contact

your corporate or governmental security officer, or seek assistance from the U.S. embassy.

ARMORED CARS AND DEFENSIVE DRIVING

In general, armored cars should be driven using the same defensive driving techniques described in chapter 10. This is especially true if you are going to be your own chauffeur. I would make one further recommendation. If you can afford an armored car you can probably afford a driver-bodyguard. This will offer you increased security and take some of the burden of defensive driving off your back. The driver-bodyguard must be professionally trained in both areas. He can pick you up and drop you off at your door and in both cases help make sure the coast is clear. A code word or signal should be established so your driver car can give you an *all clear* sign before you exit a building for the car. He can watch the car when it is parked and see that it's properly maintained. Because he is a native resident he will have a better idea of what is and is not suspicious regarding the streets, roads, other cars, and people.

Having this driver-bodyguard should not present a problem regarding your profile in most overseas areas, since they are fairly common and do not point to you as being rich or important. If this is not the case in your location then you should consider this option carefully before going ahead.

Others who will purchase an armored car may want a driver, several bodyguards, and perhaps even an escort car. If this is your desire you should seek professional help in establishing this protection since it will require a full-blown security apparatus.

Choosing a Guard

Many readers will find overseas that having a guard is not a luxury but a necessity. While their value can only be determined by your particular situation and location, it is safe to say that "if you can easily afford one then you inevitably need one." For the average American this means that if the area you are in is that poor, then the chances are that crime is high. If this is the situation, do not feel that you will look like the ugly American for displaying such an obvious need to protect your belongings.

On the contrary, you are providing someone with a job and that is no small gift in many parts of the world.

Guards come in all shapes and sizes, all colors and races. They range in quality from the fairly typical "warm body" to the highly trained and dedicated professional. While it may seem hard to believe that any guard could be described as highly trained and dedicated, reserve judgment until you have had a good one for a few years. Parting with him will give you a feeling of loss and vulnerability you did not think possible.

Whether or not to have a guard is something you will be able to decide quickly once you have arrived at your location. You don't need a set of criteria from me. But don't base your decision strictly on the basis of personal security. That may be your guard's primary function, but the majority of his pay will be earned by protecting your property.

How to go about choosing a guard will be your first concern. Contrary to what may seem logical, there are just a few set rules. After that it is really a matter of choosing the individual according to your instincts and judgment.

When possible, hire a guard yourself, rather than renting one from a company. Select only the applicant who is a trained and experienced guard. The applicant must provide references, and pass a background or security check. The person must be physically capable of performing the assigned duties, and should know how to read and write. This is important and should not be taken for granted. Other characteristics to look for are loyalty and common sense. Finally, choose a likeable applicant who genuinely wants the job, and feels this occupation is both important and meaningful.

Once you have selected a guard, you must insure that the guard understands every aspect of his job.

GUARD INSTRUCTION GUIDELINES

Clearly instruct your guard in his job duties and expected performance, in accordance with your personal security program. After an initial trial period to assess the guard's value and loyalty, you should fill him in on any essential sensitive areas of your particular program, without revealing more than absolutely necessary.

A professional, efficient, loyal guard should be treated with appropriate respect and salary. Take care of your guard and your guard will take care of you.

OFFICE-DUTY

When on duty in your office, the guard's job will be to verify the physical security of your offices, screen personnel and visitors, and act as a deterrent to armed attacks. His function in your home is more complex. He must do all those things necessary to preserve the safety of your home and family. That will require at least a basic knowledge of several chapters of this book. Carefully instruct him in these areas and make sure he understands them.

There is one last point about guards that is worth discussing in the scope of this book. Should they be armed? The answer to this problem is up to you. But if you feel the need to hire a professional guard, then he should probably be armed.

Bodyguards

Bodyguards are only for those individuals who know they are high risk targets and do not care who else knows it. Except in the case of a bodyguard/driver, bodyguards eliminate any chance you may have of maintaining a low profile. They should only be used in conjunction with a highly sophisticated and professional security program. If you need this kind of protection then you should obtain a consultant's services in setting it up, or employ a company that specializes in this type of security services.

Here is another eye-opening fact about overseas bodyguards that you should be aware of: at least 50% of all bodyguards involved in ambushes and kidnappings did nothing to help their American employers during the attack. They were bribed and paid off by the other side—your enemies. So carefully check the backgrounds of all qualified bodyguard applicants.

Remember that there is no such thing as a professional bodyguard who has not been trained by either the military, the

government, or one of a very few high quality schools. Bodyguards may be neither big nor tough, but they are smart, experienced, and highly trained. Above all they are professionals.
Being a bodyguard is not a part-time or temporary job. It is a
career. So make sure you get what you need and do not accept
second best.

Civilian Security Services
      Civilian security services can be found in most every part of
the world. They range in quality from con organizations to first
rate professional businesses. They may offer every type of security service imaginable, from supplying building guards to providing elaborate multidisciplinary security programs. They
can sell you a burglar alarm system or design a top security
building. In other words, one civilian security service or
another can provide you with almost anything you want in the
security field.
      If you need to turn to a civilian security service for help
with your security needs, make sure you choose a good one.
When you deal with a civilian security service overseas, make
sure you get the best one available and make sure they can do the
job.
      These security companies can provide you with a number
of specialized services. They can install and monitor security
systems in your home or office, and then respond to any alarms
there. If you wish, they can analyze your overseas personal
security situation, then develop a security program especially
suited to your new locale. If you are looking for a guard dog,
these companies can provide you with one. And in fact, you can
hire one of these companies to serve as private police: they can
guard you, patrol your residence, neighborhood, and office,
and even provide you with a full-time bodyguard/chauffeur.
      Finding a good civilian security service overseas should be
handled in a no nonsense manner. It is simply too important.
Talk to friends and associates. Check the local chamber of
commerce. Speak with other people who have used various
security services for their own needs and see how their choice of
companies fared for them. Go to the local police and ask their

opinion. Ask a trusted government official and get his recommendations. Find out who provides security services to banks, government, or industry. Check with the security officer at the American embassy in your location. When you pick a company, make sure they not only provide what you want but do so as a normal part of their business. Get everything guaranteed in writing, then check and double check to make sure you get what you paid for.

As you can see, a private security service can be very useful if you need one. Remember, no amount of help can replace your own personal security program. It must always remain the crux of your defense.

12
TRIPS, TRAVEL, AND VACATIONS

For many of you, one of the best aspects of overseas living will be the opportunity to travel, sightsee, and vacation in places that are close to your assignment. This may mean the next city or county, or even a nearby country. Your job may require that you travel and make business trips to places away from your main base. For whatever reason, most of you will do some traveling to other cities and countries during your tour abroad.

The fact that you will leave your home base does not mean that you can stop worrying about security. On the contrary, it means that your security planning and awareness should be increased. You may just be going from one bad situation to another. Once you have left home on a trip, be it for business or pleasure, the chances are that your security defenses will be weakened. Your understanding of the local threat situation, your familiarity with the local people, places, and customs, and your reliance on your own personal security program may all be useless at your next destination. Your arrival in a new city or country may put much of your security planning back to square one. So it is important that you not only carefully plan any trips you make, but also adhere to some basic security principles while traveling.

Where, When, and Why

When you sit down to plan your trip, consider some basic—yet important—security prerequisites. First of all you need to take a look at *where* you are going. What is the basic security situation there? If it is bad, can you change or alter your

123

plans? If your trip is for pleasure you probably should. There are plenty of other places you can visit instead that will be just as much fun, yet have few of the security drawbacks of your original destination. If it is an important business trip, maybe your client can come to you. Or maybe the trip can be postponed until things cool down. If you cannot change plans, and you will be making a trip to a problem area, you will have to take some extra security precautions.

Once you are committed to go, your first consideration will be one of *timing*. If there is a threat problem at your destination, then be sure to plan your trip when things are least likely to cause you problems. Choose dates that do not coincide with any local commemorative date or national holiday which may mark the beginning of increased civil unrest or terrorist activity. There is not likely to be joy in the streets on the dictator's birthday or the anniversary of the opposition leader's assassination.

Why you are going can have serious consequences if your trip is a diplomatic mission or major business engagement. Depending on the exact nature of this type of trip and its media coverage, you may attract the attention of a number of violent threat groups. An attack on you may not only embarrass the government but discourage others from following in your path.

Planning Your Trip

Planning your trip should begin by choosing the safest and most convenient mode of transportation to and from your destination. In terms of security, air travel is generally the best choice. Your security will rarely be a problem while en route. Car travel is somewhat more precarious. If the automobile is your chosen mode of travel, take special care to choose as safe a route as possible. Unless there is virtually no threat problem between your present location and your destination, stick to the main roads. Bypass the scenic backroads and avoid the short cuts. Stop for food and gas at the major commercial areas and avoid the "mom and pop" places. Plan your route so that overnight stops can be made in larger cities or built-up areas. Do not get lost. Use your map and ask questions when in doubt.

If the area is really dangerous, form a convoy or stick close to other traffic, and do not travel at night.

If you decide to take a bus or train, arrange for first class accommodations. Many countries offer special first class buses that provide more comfortable seating and a classier set of traveling companions. Your driver is more likely to look out for the welfare of his passengers and be conscious of security considerations, if the situation warrants it. First class accommodations on the train will make your trip more comfortable and safe. Many first class coaches on overseas trains will have attendants and be separated from cars with lower class accommodations. They may also have locking compartment doors and even security personnel.

Where to stay at your destination may be your most important consideration. In general, try to choose a first class hotel that caters to overseas visitors. These hotels have their own security personnel, and take at least some special measures to prevent trouble. Select a hotel that is as close as possible to your main area of interest or business. This will help reduce your exposure time in getting around to the places you want to go. Always select a room on a high floor. It will help keep you out of reach of any disorders on the street, and make a personal attack upon you more difficult because the attacker will have to avoid either exposure or recognition while making the lengthy trip to and from your room. Kidnapping will be even more difficult since "getting you out" without being caught may pose extreme problems. Your room itself can be given an added measure of security by using a *Port-a-lock*. A Port-a-lock can be carried with you and used on almost any standard door. It is set between the door and the frame and does not require any mounting or installation. By using one you can essentially negate the possibility of surreptitious or quick entry into your room while you are there.

Hotel lobbies should not be used for lounging or lingering since they have a history of being the scene of attacks and kidnappings.

If you use your own car to get around make sure that you drive defensively and maintain good car security. Always park your car in a safe location. In most areas overseas, the local bus system is to be avoided. It is not that you have to worry about being attacked on a bus but rather that your presence may be conspicuous to a number of unsavory elements, such as muggers and pickpockets. Subways are an excellent means of getting around most major cities but they have the same drawbacks as buses. If you do use a subway make sure you take a first class car or one occupied by a group of other people. Stay out of cars with unsavory individuals and move on to another car. If you have trouble on either a train or bus, do not hesitate to pull the emergency cord.

While it may be difficult, you should plan your security for the rest of your activities while at your destination. The extent of your planning will be directly proportional to the threat you face. If the threat is substantial, you should restrict your activities to a minimum. If it is not, you only need to be prudent about your activities. In general, be selective. Frequent only the well-known restaurants and bars. Restrict your sightseeing to the places that are well-known and well frequented. Avoid the rundown sections of town and the red light districts. If you must go to these places, have a friend who knows the area take you. Unless you know your way around, stay off the streets at night.

There is a strange phenomenon among tourists in a foreign country that has always amazed me and for which I am sure the psychologists have a good explanation. All tourists seem to be endowed with a strange sense of false security. When in a foreign country they will go places and do things that they would never do at home. They will take midnight strolls through the worst high crime areas of the city, take picnics in parks that are the uncontested domain of muggers and rapists, and think nothing at all of walking through the local red light district while wearing expensive clothes and jewelry. Whatever the reason, do not let this happen to you. If you are unfamiliar with your surroundings, ask someone you can trust for advice. Being a foreigner grants you no special immunity from crime. On the contrary, it makes you a more likely target. So do not be a victim of your own negligence.

VACATION SECURITY GUIDELINES

When traveling, plan your trip carefully—investigate the threat situation at your destination and en route if applicable. If you must travel to a high threat area, ensure that someone is waiting to meet you and has planned for your security. If warranted, armored cars and bodyguards can usually be rented from a local security service.

Make plans to maintain your home's security while you are away, and keep all aspects of your trip as confidential as possible. Maintain communication and coordination between yourself and your office, and among family members.

While at your destination, vary your schedules and routines. Make the best use of available security while keeping the lowest possible profile.

Be wary of any new contacts or friends. Do not give them any information about yourself, your family, or your trip unless you are absolutely sure they can be trusted.

13
SECURITY AND
THE FAMILY

Your personal security program is not complete until you consider how it may affect your family as individual members and as a whole. While your own security may be the most imperiled, it is your family's security that will weigh heaviest on your mind. Also, several situations exist that may be applicable to both you and your spouse, and they deserve special attention.

The Family's Role in Personal Security

Personal security is not a solitary game. It requires the help of everyone close to you, especially your family. No one can be expected to maintain constant vigilance. Nor can everyone always be expected to notice the signs of peril, even when they are obvious. Your family can play a large part in making your tour a safe and happy one. Besides assisting you directly, they can give you encouragement and understanding when the tension begins to wear on you.

Your family will have to learn to help themselves as well. You will have to be gone at least some of the time, and no amount of effort on your part will be able to provide directly for all their security needs. Spouses will have to go out on errands, children will have to go to school and play with friends, and the in-laws are bound to want the grand tour on their visit. Therefore, it is important that your family has a good knowledge of personal security as it affects them, and a thorough knowledge of your specific personal security program.

Once you have thoroughly developed your personal security program it is a good idea to sit the family down and go over it with them. Special attention should be paid to those parts that will directly affect them. Do not hesitate to be specific. If your threat situation is bad, you may want to play down some of the more severe possibilities, but do not hesitate to give them any information they will need to help with the security program. Remember, it is their program too, and they will also face at least a degree of your risk.

When considering your family's security it is worth noting that women and children generally face a substantially lower risk than men do from the violent threat. This is especially true in the case of non-criminal elements. Terrorists, urban guerrillas, revolutionary groups, and even mobs tend to avoid violent acts toward women and children. This is based on the supposition that the woman is not herself directly engaged in any activity which might in itself cause her to become a target. Acts of violence against women and children are simply not accepted by most civilized groups of people, outside of wartime situations.

This tendency is not only comforting to your peace of mind but can directly help you with your own security. For example, if the threat groups in your area are known to avoid violence against women and children, your safety may be substantially increased by having your family around. Many terrorist groups will call off an attack on a man in his car or home if they feel his wife or children might be injured in the process. In a high threat situation, having the wife run outside errands may reduce her husband's exposure rate without endangering her.

I know of at least two situations where the man was under a direct threat and used this information to save his life. In both instances the men involved had their wives answer the door while they went to a back window. In both instances terrorists had come to kidnap or assassinate the husband but were momentarily surprised when the wife answered the door. Both husbands left through back windows and made good their escapes. The wives were verbally abused by the attackers but suffered no injury of any kind. Thus, this knowledge can be useful in the right situation. However, do not overplay it. Know the violent threat and how it operates. Do not let your spouse or child become a surrogate victim.

Security: Your Own and Your Spouse's

If the husband-target has done his job, his wife should have little to worry about her own security at home. Once out of the house it may be another story. Therefore, she must have a good understanding of both car security and defensive driving. Even if she is under no threat of vehicular attack herself, she should learn to watch for surveillance and know how to handle it. Attackers can learn a lot about her husband by following her.

To the male reader: you must understand that your wife can play a large part in lowering your profile. What she does, where she goes, and who her friends are can mean the difference between a low profile and making the daily social column. Your best efforts at lowering your profile will be for naught if your wife makes a habit of having brunch with the foreign minister's wife at a fashionable French restaurant. Nor will it help if she indulges in bragging about your important job or your rich relatives. Simply put, the wife must play the same role as the husband. It may not be as much fun but it will be safer.

You and your wife's friends may not only affect your profile but could lead directly to your undoing. It is important that both of you screen your friends carefully. Be wary of anyone wanting to start a quick friendship. Pay special attention to those who seem to want to force a friendship upon you. Avoid people who seem to know more about you than they should. Never give out any personal information until you are sure of the person's authenticity and reliability. A good rule is to never confide in anybody whom you do not trust with your life.

What your wife and you do and where you go may also be important, depending on the nature and level of the threat in your area. Restrict your shopping to the major business and commercial areas. Only patronize restaurants and night clubs that are well-known, where crowds can be expected, and where security is good. Getting door-to-door service with a taxi is always a good idea for social outings. It relieves you of a lot of potential worries.

If your wife works she should also be cognizant of those security measures relevant to the office environment. She can and should play an active part in her office's security.

In many overseas cities you will find an abundance of private clubs. These clubs resemble our country or urban clubs and generally offer the same variety of activities. It is a good idea for you to have a family membership with one or more of these clubs because it will offer you, your wife, and children a place to spend your leisure time in relative security. Most of these clubs have good security since their clientele are usually from the upper class. They are generally aware of the local threat situation and take appropriate measures to ensure the safety of their members. You will find these clubs not only provide for your relaxation but will often be good for making both friends and business contacts. Although often expensive, these clubs are worth the financial investment. They are not only beneficial from a security standpoint, but will help keep your family happy on your tour and may prevent your early departure due to an unhappy home situation. Just be careful not to travel to and from your club in a set pattern or routine.

As stated previously, it is important that you get along with your servants, domestics, and guards. It is also important that your wife does. If the servants do not like her, they may not do much to help with the personal security of your family as a whole. Furthermore, they must be able to respond to her orders without hesitation in the event of an emergency. Loyal help can be a tremendous asset. Help your wife obtain their loyalty.

Without doubt, your wife can play a key role in your security and the security of your family. Keep her informed, help her, and listen to her. If she starts to take charge of your security and becomes a nag, consider yourself a lucky man. This is one time when your "back seat driver" should be heard.

Security and Your Children

Both you and your spouse have three important responsibilities regarding your children's security. You must make all the security decisions regarding their basic activities, you must teach them how to maintain their own security, and you must guide them in learning how to cope with those unknown situations where they must make their own decisions.

Talk over the security problem with your children. They must understand their responsibilities, and respect the value of your family's overall security program. Discuss your children's activities with them. Some may have to be limited, and it may be difficult to decide which activities are safe and which are not. Do not ask for too many restrictions, or you will most likely get nothing. Treat them like adults. They must know why they have to be careful in choosing their new friends and playmates; your lives may depend on it. You should also clearly define what areas are safe to play in. These areas will be your own yard, perhaps a neighbor's yard, and a nearby playground. Everything else is off limits. As with their parents, children should beware of strangers, and any suspicious activity in the neighborhood. No one in the family should accept anything from anybody who is not a close friend. This goes for gifts, rides, assistance, and so on.

Families with teen-agers may not get the neessary security cooperation from children of this age group. In this case, you may want to leave them home, or send them away to school in a safer country.

Children will spend much of their time at school. From a security standpoint, the best way to select a school is to look for one where other people, with a situation similar to your own, send their kids. Naturally, you will want to further investigate your selection on your own, and ascertain exactly what measures the school takes to maintain its students' safety.

If your children are not at home or school, they will likely be out entertaining or socializing. The theatres and restaurants that your children go to should meet the same standard security conditions that you would use. If you have any doubts about any of these places, check them out yourself.

Teaching your children to maintain their security is simply a matter of discussing the previously mentioned suggestions, and instructing them on how to behave, what to do, and what to look out for. Guiding them in learning to handle the potential unknown situation is a matter of imparting good common sense. Children are generally smarter than most adults give them credit for, and their ability to make the right decision at the right time can be downright astounding. Help them learn to make decisions and give them confidence in their ability to make the right choice. Do not be surprised if they enjoy the tour more than you do. Chances are they will adapt quickly and learn the language in no time. Then you can suffer the common embarrassment of having your six-year-old translate for you.

Other Family Considerations

There are a few situations which may apply to one or more members of your family and yet affect the security of everyone. Make sure they are handled with care.

Some situations start off involving one or more family members and end up affecting everyone's security.

Personal and family arguments should never be carried to any extremes. Security is shattered when spouses storm out of the house and children run away from home. Everyone should understand that family security takes priority over personal problems.

With this priority in mind, family members should co-ordinate a communication system. Keeping each other posted on a sign-out board is one simple safety measure. Individual activities and family plans should be reviewed for possible problems.

Be aware that local disputes with native residents have a way of becoming unpredictably unpleasant. Avoid them in the first place. If an explosive situation does develop, do not get involved. Leave the scene immediately or notify the necessary officials.

The same caution must be extended to *any* exposure through the media. Stay away from photographers and interviewers. Even incidental publicity can spell trouble overseas.

Security and Sex

No book on security and overseas living would be complete without mentioning sex. While this may seem a bit absurd, it is quite the contrary. Mistresses, affairs, weekend flings, and plain old adultery are common fare for Americans living overseas, both husbands and wives. A variety of reasons explains why these kinds of sexual escapades seem to increase in the overseas environment: a high degree of social contact, increased partying, a greater sense of community among Americans, boredom, and opportunity are just a few. Why or whether these occurrences take place is not my concern. It is *how* they take place that can seriously affect your personal security.

An extramarital relationship with a foreigner can cause you many problems, unless you do some careful planning. Every little "adventure" must be handled in such a way that your security program remains intact. Slipping out the back door in the middle of the night to see your paramour may defeat all your efforts toward good security. I know of one executive who lost his life because of this hasty maneuver. He had one of the most elaborate security setups that money could buy.

Here is some advice for readers who cannot resist temptation. To begin with, men should always be wary of sexy, mysterious women who quickly succumb to their charms. These types are probably interested in more than charm and good looks. The reverse situation holds true for women readers as well.

The bottom line is to know your partner. Make sure your partner's interest in you is not really an attempt to gather information or lure you into a trap. For hundreds of years, various violent elements have used this gimmick—usually with great success. Another ugly possibility, extortion and blackmail, is also a source of concern.

After a period of time, you may feel that you can trust your partner. It is best to resist this temptation. So as a general rule, never give your partner any personal information about you, your family, or your security program.

When you do meet with your paramour, be sure that the location is secure, and that a close friend will know where to contact you. This close friend should be told about your relationship, and directed to call the police if it ever appears that you have been set up.

Finally, be certain that your absence is credibly explained so that your family will not start a premature house-to-house search for you. More than one man has lied to his wife about going to so-and-so's, only to have his wife scream "Kidnapping!" when she discovered he did not arrive there.

While these measures will give you some help in watching your security when engaging in extramarital affairs, they will by no means provide you any guarantees. The best solution of course, is simply to abstain from these types of relationships. If you cannot, then look for a partner who is American or someone you have known well for a long time.

No matter what the circumstances, use your head. Sex is perhaps one of humanity's greatest vulnerabilities and the people who play dirty will not hesitate to use it to your detriment. So do not become a victim of one of the oldest con games on earth.

One last note. Your teen-agers have the same vulnerabilities as you do. If they engage in sex, and you should always assume they do, make sure they understand the importance of screening their partners in terms of security. They too can be a bounty of information to those who would plan your kidnapping or death.

PART III

VICTIM

"No one is ever completely immune from becoming the victim of a violent act. No amount of care, planning, or security can guarantee that you are completely safe from the hostile forces that may surround you. Therefore, you must be prepared for the worst. Also, there may be family members to worry about besides yourself. Your responsibility to your family continues whether you survive or not."

14
PREPARING FOR THE WORST

Preparing for the worst is a matter of facing reality. While you are overseas there is at least a remote possibility that you may be kidnapped or killed. Because of this you must make plans and preparations to ensure that your family is taken care of and that they know what to do in the event this happens. Most of these plans and preparations are standard measures that you would undertake simply in case of natural death. However, there are a few special actions you will need to perform in order to cover the unusual nature of the potential situation. It may be unpleasant to discuss these actions but it is necessary.

Preparations

A will is an obvious necessity in the event of your death, and is a preparation you probably already made long ago. Not having one can cause extreme complications, especially in the overseas situation. Have a will filed with a lawyer or relative in the United States. Have a certified copy with you in your foreign location. Along the same lines, a power of attorney can be very useful in the event you are kidnapped. It will give your spouse or family the means to handle your legal affairs while you are being held. You should also give a power of attorney to your lawyer, relative, or close friend back in the United States. This person will be better located to handle legal necessities than will your family overseas. Your family also may not be up to it.

Whether or not you are married, it is important that the people for whom you work be aware of your *legal* next of kin.

Too often individuals assume that their employers are automatically aware of this when in fact they are not.

You should also ensure that all your important papers and documents are stored in a safe place, and that someone else is aware of this location. This document cache will help your family or employer take care of all necessary legal matters. These papers should include any legal documents, trusts, wills, powers of attorney, deeds, titles, insurance papers, stocks, bonds, bank records, and so on.

Personal funds, bank accounts, and savings accounts will become very important in the event you are kidnapped or killed. If you are killed your spouse and family may have to live on these limited funds until your will is probated. If you are kidnapped, they may have to survive on these funds for the entire time you are held. So make sure that they will have immediate legal access to these funds in either event. Be certain that there is enough money in these funds to tide them over for several months.

The need for these previous preparations is probably obvious to you. This next one may not be. It is important that you have a complete and accurate set of medical records with you at your foreign post. Medical records are not only valuable in case of sickness or hospitalization, but can be an important record if you are kidnapped. These records provide the authorities with your physical description and other identifying features, an idea of your current physical state, what you can stand up to, how long you can go, and what special medicines you might need. At least some of their actions will be dependent upon this information. Make sure your medical file includes a current picture of yourself.*

You may be wondering about the value of kidnap insurance as a preparation. Kidnap insurance is now available to most anyone who can afford it, and it is expensive. The insurance will usually cover up to any amount you specify and will

---

*You should always maintain current pictures and medical records for each member of your family.

be applicable to any type of kidnapping that takes place, so long as it meets the terms of the contract. In addition, the insurance often offers a specified amount to be paid to your family while you are being held.

In principle, kidnap insurance is a tacit surrender to all kidnappers, be they terrorists or criminals. On this basis I do not recommend it. However, realities being what they are, you may feel discretion is the better part of valor and that the insurance is worthwhile. If you decide to take out kidnapping insurance, try to get your employer to pay the bill. The amount of insurance you will need depends upon the history of ransoms paid to kidnappers in your threat area. When talking to the insurance company, do not ask what previous kidnappers requested for ransom sums; ask what they were paid. The difference is usually substantial. Your policy should then be based upon the higher side of previously paid ransoms. $250,000 might not sound like much when you hear through the media of so many astronomical sums being paid out. But who would throw away that much money and kill you just to prove a point? Very few people indeed.

If you do decide to take out kidnap insurance, the insurance company will go into much greater detail than I have on what the different aspects of your policy mean. One favorable point regarding kidnap insurance is that it may give you and your family more peace of mind. The bad point is that this peace of mind may result in slack security practices, which *can get you kidnapped.*

Planning

Once you have completed your basic preparations you will need to do some contingency planning. It will be very helpful to both your family and your company if they have some idea of what you want done in the event of an incident. What is needed is a set of specific plans regarding actions that should be taken following your kidnapping or death. Here are some basic questions to ask yourself before starting your overseas tour.

IF YOU ARE KIDNAPPED:

Immediate actions—Should your family stay in the country or return to the United States? Should they try to raise a ransom or not? Should they be involved in negotiating your release? Should they contact the authorities or go it alone? What other friends or relatives do you want contacted?

What should your employer do? How can others help your family? What business associate do you want to liaison with your family while you are being held? Do you want your employer to handle your affairs and supervise any negotiations? To whom should they pay your salary if you are not married?

Secondary actions—Should your family members improve their security and in what way? Should they talk to the press or other media? Should they be willing to make political statements or not? Should they seek the assistance of any important political figures and if so, whom? What should they do if you are held for an extended period of time? How should they borrow money and from whom? Should they encourage the police or other authorities to release you by force or should they try to forestall such action? If your spouse works should he or she continue working? Should your children continue in school? What code words can you use when contacting your family to tell them you are safe, the general location of where you're being held, if the kidnappers intend to kill you whether the ransom is paid or not, or if the police are getting close?

What actions can your employers take in the long run to help your family? What actions should they take to financially support your family? Should they pay a ransom themselves or push the police to try and find you?

The answers to most of these questions are essentially matters for you to decide. There are only a few points I would recommend. All non-essential members of your family should leave the country as soon as possible. This will generally mean that only your spouse need stay behind to help the police or negotiators. If not needed, your spouse should leave too. This will relieve a lot of your anxiety, since many kidnappers will threaten to take actions against the rest of your family if a ransom is not quickly paid.

It is also essential that your family immediately contact the local authorities as soon as they receive knowledge of your kidnapping. They should also contact the local American embassy and your employer.

It is a very good idea for you to find a friend or fellow employee who will take care of your family and other matters for you while you are being held. This individual should be someone you and your family know well and someone you trust. He or she can be a real help to you and your family during this time of crisis.

IF YOU ARE ASSASSINATED:

Immediate actions—Should your family leave immediately? Should they hold any kind of local service? How should remembrances be directed? Where should your family move? Should they talk to the press or media? Should they offer a reward for the capture of your attackers? What action should they expect from your employers? What other special instructions do you want carried out?

What should your employers do? How can they best help your family? Who would you want to act as liaison between them and your family? How would you want the company to handle the public information?

Secondary actions—These actions should be the same as those you would take when planning for a natural death. It is simply a matter of imparting your hopes and desires for the future to your loved ones.

Missing Overseas

While we have discussed kidnapping and assassination, there is still one more category that needs to be touched upon: that of *missing*. While the term *missing person* in the United States has a number of not so serious possible explanations, it can be quite different in some areas overseas. This is especially true if you will live in an area where open guerrilla warfare is raging.

You should take this into consideration and make sure that your family, and perhaps your employers, know what to do if you turn up missing. It is a small item but it should be taken seriously. There may be no greater suffering for a family than to have the fate of a loved one go unknown. Planning and preparation for this on your part may not ease the pain but it will help solve some of the immediate problems of what to do.

15
HANDLING THREATS, EXTORTION, AND ATTACKS

Your personal conduct in the event of a threat, extortion, or attack will directly affect the outcome of that situation. How you act, how you react, or whether you act at all will mean the difference between being on the winning or losing side.

While every threat, extortion, and attack situation will be somewhat different, there are basic defensive concepts and ideas that may be appropriate to each of these situations. These concepts do not represent hard and fast rules, nor should they be thought of as specific guidelines. They are defensive possibilities that should be given your thoughtful consideration and applied when necessary, in a manner that is appropriate to your needs and realistic to the situation. Above all they must be tempered to your individual character and ability.

To effectively use the information in this chapter it is important that you have a good knowledge of the following points:

- The threat situation in your area.
- The threat groups in your area that may affect you.
- The methods of threat, extortion, and attack used by the threat group in your area.

- An idea of how successful the above methods have been.
- A good introspective knowledge of yourself.

With this knowledge you will have a reasonable basis for making some plans and decisions in regard to potential threat, extortion, or attack situations. Naturally, it is somewhat optimistic to suppose that these plans will be both applicable and effective in every situation every time. However, they will give you a basic framework to start from, and that in itself can be very important. Having given previous consideration to your actions in the event of one of these situations, you will be able to better understand what you are up against, what potential actions you might take, what actions would be inappropriate, and how you can best react to the situation in order to survive.

Let's take an example. Shortly after arriving at your overseas location you do a basic threat analysis. You discover that a terrorist group called Omega X is operating in your area and that they are targetting against Americans. You also learn that the group primarily engages in kidnappings using vehicular attacks. In the past these attacks have been very violent, but were poorly planned and often unsuccessful. You further learn that Omega X is the only group that operates in this manner and against Americans. You learn from the U.S. Embassy that Omega X has killed most of its American kidnapping victims due to outrageous demands that must inevitably go unmet. Also, the local government has just announced that it will no longer negotiate with Omega X and will prosecute anyone else who tries, regardless of the circumstances.

Given this situation, what would you plan to do in the event of vehicular attack? Obviously your conduct in the event of such an attack should be largely influenced by the information you have at hand. Your preplanning is thus largely a process of deductive reasoning.

You know, for instance, that any vehicular attack upon you is probably the work of Omega X, and that such an attack is probably aimed at an attempted kidnapping. You also know that few of the previous American victims have survived such kidnappings. You must further consider that the local government has established a new policy that will make dealing with the kidnappers even harder for those who might seek to help you or pay your ransom. Finally, you know that these vehicular attacks are poorly planned and often unsuccessful.

Based upon this reasoning it would seem like a good idea to try every means available of beating the attack attempt and escaping, even if this will put you in some danger of being killed. The logic is simply a matter of playing the odds. You might as well take a chance on trying to get away if in all probability you are going to be killed if the kidnapping is successful.

From this example you can see that a little research and preparation can be helpful in an attack situation. The real life attack situations you may be faced with might not present such clear-cut or obvious preplanning options. Essentially, you should make the best use of all the information that is available, plan to the degree that you can, and be prepared to make quick decisions.

Defensive Concepts

As stated previously, there are some ideas and concepts that have defensive applications to the various threat, extortion, and attack situations you may face. Let's look at them:

THREATS

A threat is generally a pronounced statement to the effect that someone is going to hurt or punish you. Threats may range from the intimidating screams of a crowd yelling "Yankee go home!" to a carefully crafted note from a terrorist group informing you that you will soon be assassinated. How a threat may affect you will depend upon what the threat is, who is making it, and what the perpetrator's ability is to carry it out. An important point to note is that a threat is nothing but words unless it can be carried out by the perpetrator.

While all threats should be taken seriously, they must also be handled in a rational and realistic manner. Over-reaction is as bad as no reaction at all.

Americans overseas are often the target of threats. Most of the time these threats will not constitute a real danger and can be handled in a routine manner. Occasionally, a threat will present very serious implications and must be handled with the greatest of care. You will therefore have to know how to differentiate the serious threats from the ones that are not.

The reason that threats are used against Americans is that the threat is a fairly effective, yet safe, way of intimidating the American living overseas and provoking him to return home.

Whether or not you decide to be intimidated and return home may depend on your ability to plan effectively for threats and handle them when they arise. Usually, the threats that will be significant to you are the ones that will either come as no surprise, or that make no attempt to hide the identity of the threatener. So, if you live in a terrorist environment, are a known potential target, and receive a threat from a particular terrorist group, you should not be shocked. Scared yes, but not shocked. If you have done your homework you should know how serious this threat really is, whether it can and will be carried out, and what you can do about it. On the other hand, you may receive a threat from the local witchdoctor and be completely baffled, as happened to an acquaintance of mine. In this case you will probably choose to ignore it and not give it a second thought. This is exactly what my friend did, much to the surprise of his native neighbors.

Planning for threats is a matter of preselecting those groups that present a serious danger to your safety, then deciding what you will do if they threaten you. While your courses of action are many and varied, there is a basic procedure to follow. When you receive a serious and *valid* threat from a known threat group you should be prepared to take immediate steps to increase your overall security program. Your family should know what steps to take to help you accomplish this and also to further protect themselves. You should immediately inform the local authorities, assuming that they are not the originators, and the U.S. Embassy. Your employers should be advised of the threat and informed of any actions you plan to take. If the threat is serious and is against your life, you must *immediately* change all your basic routines. Threats of this nature will usually be carried out quickly since they depend on a known ability to get to you even after you are forewarned.

If the threat is not to be taken seriously, then you can file it away. A security expert should make this decision, not you. If it is to be taken seriously, then act upon it immediately and prepare yourself for what may come. Whatever you do, make every attempt to settle the issue in your mind and in reality. Threats are designed to intimidate you and cause you mental anguish, whether or not they will be carried out. Do not let this happen. Your mental health is just as important as your physical health is.

EXTORTION

In many ways extortion and threats have a lot in common. Extortion is a means of obtaining money, property, promises, or specific actions from you by means of threats, force, coercion, or fraud. In other words if you yield to a threat, you have been successfully subjected to extortion.

Extortion is not an uncommon practice against Americans overseas, especially in the business sector. Your first encounter with it may come when you try to get your household goods. If you do not come through with a bribe for the local customs official or freight forwarder you may be informed that your goods will be held up on the dock for several months. Unless you are a saint you will probably part with a few bottles of Scotch or some other bribe and await the prompt arrival of your goods. If this happens, you have been successfully extorted.

The above case is mild and represents an age-old custom in some countries. No amount of American idealism or U.S. government regulation is likely to change it. However, there are many more serious ways in which extortion can have a profound effect upon your safety. If you live in an area of open hostilities you may have to pay extortion money, or "insurance," to one or more of the hostile groups in order to be left alone or insured safe conduct in the area. Your business may also suffer the same fate. Naturally, paying extortion to one group may make you the enemy of another. Regardless of how it emanates, extortion is serious business and should be given careful attenton. Planning ahead of time for extortion is a matter of knowing what types of extortion practices are prominent in your area and how they might affect your safety. This is best done by getting some help from security experts or trustworthy friends who have extensive experience in your locale. They will know what to look for, how serious the extortion threat is, and how it may affect your safety. They can tell you what they and others have done to handle it and what your options may be. Get as much information as you can and be prepared to handle extortion when confronted with it. Always try to be as legal and ethical as you can, but do not be stupid. When appropriate, go to the authorities and try to get them to help you. Unfortunately, in some countries they are often the perpetrators of petty extortion. Always inform the U.S. embassy of the extortion attempt, even if you must do so on a "deniable" basis in order to avoid potential legal problems with your own government. While they may not be able to condone your actions, they will likely understand them and very much appreciate the information. If the extortion involves a major business deal, they may be able to help you by confronting the local government with the facts of your case.

If you face extortion of a more personal nature, be prepared to play tough and say "no." If you let yourself become the victim of an extortion once, you are likely to have to face it again and again.

To sum up, never allow a successful extortion effort to take place if at all possible. If you must, than make sure you know what you are doing, what the stakes are, and what consequences you may face. Unless it is a case of petty extortion it is best to refuse to cooperate and if necessary, pack your bags and go home.

The Attack Situation

As mentioned earlier, your conduct in the event of an attack can play a large role in determining whether or not you survive it. How you handle yourself in an attack situation can be at least partially preplanned if you have done your homework. Start by considering the most likely types of attack situations you might face. It may be from terrorists or guerrillas. It is more likely that it will come from either the criminal element or members of a riot action that is the result of general civil disorder. In each case there are some things you can do to better your chances of surviving an attack situation.

TERRORISTS

Refer back to the beginning of this chapter for suggestions on how to handle yourself in the event of a true terrorist attack. Terrorist techniques and methods of attack will differ from group to group and area to area. There are, however, some general characteristics of all terrorist attacks that are worth examining. Any terrorist attack upon you that is not almost immediately successful may offer you a good chance to escape or evade capture/assassination. Terrorist attacks are designed to work like a small scale blitzkrieg. They are dependent upon split second timing and execution. Anything that throws off this timing or impedes the execution may be to your great advantage. Another key feature to terrorist attacks is coordination. If all members of the terrorist attack do not coordinate their actions exactly as planned, there will probably be a gap in their trap. This gap, if recognized, may provide your means of escape.

The key element involved in defeating a terrorist attack is delaying the successful execution of their attack. If you can delay the attackers and make them take more time than they have planned for, they will eventually break off the attack because they will have to escape themselves. Also, if you can escape from the immediate area of the attack it is highly unlikely the attackers will pursue you.

If you should decide to try to defeat a terrorist attack that may take place upon you then remember this: be prepared for the unexpected and do the unexpected. They will attack you when you are least prepared and you must react in a manner for which they are least prepared.

CRIMINALS

Preparing to handle a criminal attack is simply a matter of doing some basic research and using common sense. Find out how the violent criminal elements operate, what type of crimes they engage in, and when and under what conditions they resort to violence. Pay special attention to the criminal element that may well affect you. For instance, do burglars become violent if caught or confronted? If so, it may be best to call the police and stay in bed rather than risk a confrontation in the dark. Do street robbers or holdup men use violence if necessary to get your money? If so, hand it over quickly. Will a thief cut off your finger to get your ring if he has to? Then do not wear rings that are hard to take off easily.

Your primary concern with the criminal element is to determine when, and when not, to resist. As always, your actions should reflect a desire to protect your life rather than your property.

The criminal-terrorist should normally be viewed in the same light as a terrorist. However, there are differences and they should be noted. Criminal terrorists often do not return their kidnapping victims alive, regardless of whether a ransom is paid. They may be more apt to use extreme violence or torture to gain your cooperation or make you perform specific actions. Ultimately, their motivation is money and not politics. If criminal terrorists are active in your area, study them and learn how best to handle their attacks.

MOBS AND RIOTERS

Mob action, rioters, and general civil unrest are all real and pertinent threats to many Americans living overseas. Planning for these contingencies is no small matter. In general, your entire security program will contribute to how well you prepare yourself for the unpleasant realities of a breakdown of law and order. Where you live, who your friends are, who you work for, and what your profile is, are just a few of the things that may determine the effects these situations will have upon you. Your plan regarding these contingencies need not be elaborate. Usually, but not always, you will have some advance warning that the local civil order situation is deteriorating, and that a riot may occur.

If a mob action does occur, you and your family should first get off the streets, and go home and stay there. For this reason, keep a stockpile of extra food and sundries at your home. While there maintain contact with other Americans, close native friends, your employer, and the U.S. Embassy.

Should your home be in a threat area, consider staying with a trusted friend, or at a first-class international hotel.

If you must go out in public, avoid areas of known unrest. Also make sure that you are not easily identified as being an American. This includes parking your American car (if you have one) in a safe garage until the civil disorder is over.

16
SURVIVING THE KIDNAP OR HOSTAGE SITUATION

To many of you the title of this chapter may seem a bit silly, since your survival in a kidnap or hostage situation would seem to be completely dependent upon everyone else but you. Your kidnappers, the police, and those who may pay your ransom would all appear to have a much larger voice in whether you survive the ordeal. In many instances, this is not the case. Quite possibly *you* will play the most significant part in determining how the incident is resolved. You, your personality, your attitudes, actions, and behavior will often make the difference between an unpleasant ending or one which you will be able to tell your grandchildren about in your old age. Do not underestimate your role. You *can* make a difference.

Kidnappers and Hostage-Takers

What manner of people, you may ask here, would use your life as a bargaining tool to obtain money, notoriety, or political concessions? We know they may be labeled as terrorists, revolutionaries, guerrillas, or simply criminals. But going beyond these labels, consider that they are all human beings, and as human beings they have personalities, feelings, emotions, and sometimes a sense of morality. All of these characteristics are the result of, and the reason for, contact between themselves and other people. *Contact* is the key word. They have reacted, do react, and will react to contact with their fellow man. The more contact they have, the more these human characteristics come into play.

In most cases, if you are a kidnap victim or hostage you will have contact with one or more of your abductors. This contact will result in some degree of human interaction. It is this interaction, combined with some basic survival techniques that can help you live to tell about your experience.

The type of hostage-taker or kidnapper that you encounter may vary considerably in age, intelligence, background, and personality. Some will be ruthless and totally unconcerned whether you live or die. Others may be sensitive and idealistic, almost apologetic that you had to be their victim. Whatever category they fit in, they can usually be affected to some extent by the actions you take after you have been kidnapped. Naturally, there are those who will not hesitate to kill you despite any personal feelings they may have developed for you. These are usually the more extreme terrorists or the hardened criminals. But many more can be affected by their contact with you and may have second thoughts about executing you if that becomes called for. Whatever type of individual you face, make sure that all your efforts are aimed at avoiding his ire and gaining his compassion.

The Attack and Kidnapping

You may be amazed at how rapid and how violent your abduction may be. You may have no time to resist or even react. Events may speed by you and the whole episode appear dream-like. This is normal and is the usual pattern found in both kidnappings and hostage-takings. The victim is usually so overwhelmed by the event that he will often appear paralyzed and unable to perform the simplest of acts.

The abduction itself will have followed a carefully laid plan designed to maximize the abductors' chances of success and minimize your chances of resistance or escape. Most kidnappings follow a set routine as listed on the next page:

1. Selection of the victim(s).
2. Intelligence gathering.
3. Surveillance of the victim and his routines.
4. Formation of an attack plan.
5. The attack and capture.
6. Movement of the victim to a safe location.
7. Holding the victim.
8. Negotiation and/or propaganda.
9. Movement of the victim to a new location.
10. Resolution of the episode.

While the kidnapping routine may vary, most will follow this basic routine. Some kidnappers will not move you at all once you are held in a seemingly safe location. Most terrorists will move you several times in order to ensure maximum security. The type and amount of negotiating can vary considerably. The amount of time you are held may be determined as much by your propaganda value as your ransom. Whether, when, and how you are set free will depend entirely upon the particular circumstances of your situation.

Unlike kidnappings, hostage-taking is often aimed at capturing a particular place, location, or means of transportation, in addition to taking hostages. While the attack may be directed to capture a certain type of hostage, the individual hostages themselves are not normally pre-selected or targetted. So far as you will be concerned, hostage-taking is usually a political act designed to further the attackers' particular cause.

The Typical Terrorist Kidnapping

In order to help you prepare for the potentiality that you might be kidnapped, it is worth taking a look at what you might expect. The following kidnapping is fairly typical of many terrorist groups around the world. The techniques are no big secret and most terrorist groups employ these basic methods in their kidnappings.

You may be walking to your office, leaving the local grocery store, driving your car, or doing any one of a hundred things which are part of a routine that put you in a position to be attacked. Without even realizing what has happened you are being dragged into a car. You are probably being hit, kicked, and yelled at in a most vicious manner. You are constantly being ordered and are physically abused if you do not instantly obey. The first chance you have to think is while lying on the back floor of a car. Your mind is a blur and you have trouble trying to gather your thoughts. You finally understand that you have been kidnapped and you are scared silly. Your first thoughts concern your very survival. You wonder if you are going to die. You will likely be concerned about your family. Every so often you may be physically abused (but not badly) and yelled at. This is to keep you from gathering your thoughts and get you to react quickly and consistently to the orders of your abductors. At some point during this ride you may be gagged, tied, and blindfolded. After a short time (which may seem an eternity) you will be dragged out of the car and pushed into another one. By now you will be thinking a little more clearly. The chances are you will not ever think of escaping but only wonder what will happen next. After a time you will be dragged from the car again and moved quickly inside a house or building. You will notice that your captors have been joined by other comrades.

Once you are safely in the hideout you will probably be stripped and searched. If you are stripped you will feel completely defenseless (a common reaction). You may be shoved around, questioned, verbally abused, or made fun of. In a short time you will be locked away in a room, attic, basement, or behind a wall. Chances are you will have some time to yourself since your captors will wish to verify that their escape was successful and to discuss or celebrate their success.

Now is the waiting time. You may be moved again and taken to a new hideout but the following routine will probably be the same in any case.

You will be interrogated by your captors, but it is unlikely that you will be brutalized. You will occasionally suffer more indignities but after a time they will have less effect upon you. You will be kept isolated most of the time and will only have contact with one or two guards on a regular basis. After the first few days you will begin to converse with these guards and you may even engage in a game of cards.

During this holding period you will suffer a great deal of mental anguish and depression. You will continue to worry about your family. You will be angry at yourself for having allowed yourself to be kidnapped. You will fear for your life and be anxious about what is happening and what will happen. You will want to know as much as possible about any negotiations that are going on and what the outlook seems to be. If you are held for more than a few days your physical and mental health may begin to deteriorate. You may also find yourself becoming angry at your friends, family, the police, or your employers for not having arranged for your release. You may begin to take the kidnappers' side and in some cases you will feel more akin to them than your own family. The longer you are held the more likely you are to become friendly or even involved with your abductors. You may even begin to see your own abduction as a logical and reasonable act by well meaning people.

All of this will change the moment your release has been arranged. You will again think of yourself as a prisoner and your captors will do the same.

After your release you will feel a tremendous exhilaration which may be followed by deep depression or anxiety. With medical help you will shortly come out of it.

The above description of a kidnapping is by no means a conclusive account of all the possibilities. It should give you some idea of what you can expect and what is common to many terrorist kidnappings. The details were drawn from a number of actual terrorist kidnappings and they appear as common denominators in the majority of these cases.

Kidnapping/Hostage Survival Suggestions
While each kidnapping or hostage situation will be unique, there are some basic and simple measures you can take to maximize your prospects for survival. All of these measures are practicable and should not in any way adversely effect your situation.

To begin with, *immediately following the attack,* do not resist once you have been captured. It will serve no purpose but to further aggravate your situation. Obey your captors' demands quickly and to the letter. This will minimize your chances of being beaten or injured. Try to remain calm and quiet. This will help calm your abductors and reduce the chance that they will act irrationally towards you. You want to avoid injury, since a broken arm or rib may go untreated for weeks.

Upon arrival at your place of detention, try to regain your self control. Erratic behavior on your part may result in the same behavior on the part of your abductors. At this time, inform your captors of any injuries, medical problems, or medicinal needs you have. The sooner these problems are taken care of, the better. And once again, remain passive and do not ask questions. Your abductors will have enough on their minds. Additional pressures may spark a violent reaction.

After you are settled in your place of detention, collect your thoughts and evaluate your situation. It is important that you start thinking clearly, calmly, and rationally as soon as possible. Start to look for ways of escape. This must be done secretly, of course. Escape may be difficult or impossible but you should not miss a good opportunity if it occurs. Also, plan your actions carefully and avoid instinctive acts. The spontaneous act of returning a blow for a blow may cost you your life. Keep busy with mental activity, and avoid depression. Mental lethargy and depression are the first steps to mental deterioration. It may not seem important here, but learn to manage your time. Make yourself a daily schedule and follow it as much as possible. It will help you to keep your morale up. This includes practicing your religious faith. Your routine should also include doing physical exercise every day, and maintaining your hygiene to the extent possible. Your physical well-being is of obvious importance.

When it comes to *handling your kidnappers,* feel your way carefully. Find out what your kidnappers are like and act in a manner that will meet with their approval. An image of hostility will only result in harsher treatment and eliminate your chances of gaining sympathy. Try to gain your kidnappers' respect. Your abductors may not like you or what you stand for but if they respect you as a person it can be of great advantage. Your abductors may try and involve you in polemic discussions. These are to be avoided. If you must engage in such discussions, tailor your comments so as not to offend or incite your abductors.

A special word of caution here: be very careful of all female abductors and any males who appear mentally deficient or unstable. These are the people who are most prone to violence and erratic or sadistic behavior.

On the other hand, when possible, establish bonds and become friendly with those kidnappers who appear receptive. *This is very important!* Simply put, it is hard for most people to injure or kill anyone they have grown to know and like.

If you are interrogated, avoid discussing secrets or any other information which might be useful to your abductors. Such information will only reinforce your abductors' opinion as to your value as a victim.

Should a ransom negotiation process begin, do not *ever* tell your abductors that their ransom demands can or cannot be met. Such actions will only interfere with your negotiators. Furthermore, you must avoid discussing any specific issues regarding the negotiations. If in doubt, play dumb. Such discussions will have the same result as stated above. While involved in the negotiations, do not let yourself become a pawn of their propaganda. Helping them with their propaganda effort may only result in a more lengthy captivity so you can continue to "help" in these efforts. You should also try to help your abductors stay optimistic about the negotiations. If they decide that continued negotiations are useless, your life may be forfeited.

Treat lengthy negotiations as normal and be sure your abductors see that you are not surprised at the delay. Lengthy negotiations are common and if you understand this, so may your abductors. Do not be alarmed if negotiations appear to have broken down. They will likely resume. Kidnap negotiations are akin to union contract negotiations. Everyone will stall as long as possible to get the best deal.

If at any time you are allowed to contact your family or authorities, use your pre-arranged "code words" to signal your well-being, location, and your abductors' intentions. This can both reassure your family and help the local authorities hasten your rescue.

If a rescue attempt takes place, be prepared for it. Have a plan of action and be prepared to put it into effect at a moment's notice. This plan should include avoiding obvious lines of fire and possible assault routes that would be used by your rescuers. Hide behind protective furniture if possible or stay on the floor. Your captors may attempt to execute you or your rescuers may accidentally shoot you. Also, help your rescuers in any way possible. Let them know exactly where you are. Point out your captors' positions if possible. Lastly, be prepared to run for it if the rescue stalls. Do not wait for your rescuers to reach you. Escape as soon as possible to avoid the possibility of being executed by your captors.

After your release, help the police as soon as you are able. You have a moral obligation to help the authorities capture and prosecute your abductors. Rest and recuperate until you have physically recovered from the ordeal. You will need it more than you think. Do not hesitate to seek psychiatric help if you are having problems readjusting. Many kidnap and hostage victims need help in returning to normal lives. Help your family recover as well. They will have suffered too.

Finally, make sure your security is improved so you will not have to go through this ordeal again. At least one business-man has been kidnapped twice by the same terrorist group. Naturally, the second ransom was larger than the first.

By closely following these suggestions you will maximize your chances of survival. Regardless of how things may appear to be going, try to keep a good attitude and make the best of the situation. If you survive the first three days the chances are excellent that you will eventually be released. No matter what your captors tell you, be assured that a lot of people are trying hard to arrange your release.

PART IV

APPENDIX

"Self-preservation is the first law of nature."

S. Butler
Remains, 1675

17
SECURITY
PROGRAM
CHECKLISTS

By now you should have a firm grasp of what a personal security program is, what it can mean to you and your family, and what you can do to create an effective one. Yet you wll have derived little benefit from having read this book unless you use it to develop a sound personal security program for yourself and family. Putting it off or "playing the odds" may lead to a great misfortune.

The checklists that follow are designed to verify the completeness of your program, and provide a convenient outline for your planning. As is obvious from the nature of this book, they cannot alone be used to develop a personal security program.

Review these lists carefully and mark those items that are relevant to your own situation. If you are unable to answer or do not fully understand any of the questions you have marked, refer back to the relevant passages in the book.

When you are familiar with all the pertinent checklist items, and have acted upon the appropriate portions, then you will have developed your own personal security program. By making that program a part of your daily life, you will achieve a level of security vastly superior to that which most other Americans overseas have attained. You will also find your tour abroad a much more fruitful and enjoyable one for you and your family.

Best of luck, and *bon voyage!*

Checklist #1

SOURCES OF
SECURITY INFORMATION

1. Your own company or employer.
2. Other American companies that operate in your overseas location.
3. The media and publications.
4. The Department of State.
5. The Department of Commerce.
6. The local American embassy.
7. The local American consulate.
8. The local government.
9. The local police and security services.
10. Americans with extensive living experience in the area.

DETERMINING
THE THREAT

1. General economic, social, and political situation in the country?
2. Current stability of the country?
3. Past and current levels of violence?
4. Probability of continued or increased violence?
5. Ability of the local government to handle the violence?
6. Groups or elements that may present a violent threat, especially to Americans?
    A. Type of group?
    B. Size and composition of group?
    C. Type and magnitude of threat presented?
    D. Group's method of operation?
    E. Group's method of targetting?
    F. Specific details of violent actions group has directed at Americans?
7. Degree of support for these groups by the local population?
8. General feeling towards Americans in the country?
9. General level of violent threat towards Americans?
10. Probability of you becoming a target?
11. Personal characteristics that would make you a target?

Checklist #3

LOWERING YOUR PROFILE

1. Can you avoid the public limelight?
2. Can you sufficiently play down your financial status or image?
3. Can and do you avoid all aspects of an ostentatious lifestyle?
4. Can you avoid the media?
5. Do you avoid other people who may themselves be a target?
6. Do you avoid discussing information or interests which may raise your profile?
7. Are you a friend of everyone and an enemy of no one?

Checklist #4

RESIDENTIAL SECURITY

1. Selecting a home
   A. Safest location?
   B. Safest type of dwelling (house, apartment, etc.)?
   C. Solid construction that meets good security standards?
2. Limiting access to the house.

Doors
   A. Solid doors with good locks?
   B. At least two pin tumbler type locks on each door one of which is a deadbolt?
   C. Peepholes on all exterior doors?
   D. Bars or grilles to protect any glass doors?
   E. Sturdy door frames?
   F. Doors fits snugly into frame?
   G. Doors kept locked at all times?

Windows
   A. All windows of sturdy construction?
   B. Windows fit snugly into frame?
   C. Sturdy window frames?
   D. All windows have key-type locks?
   E. Window bars or grilles where necessary?
   F. All windows have curtains?
   G. All windows locked and curtains closed except when necessary?

Other Entrances
   A. All other exterior entrances secure (garage doors, crawl spaces, coal chutes, etc.)?
   B. All of sturdy construction?
   C. All have key-type locks?

       D. All barred, grilled or reinforced as necessary?

Walls, Fences, and Gates

       A. Walls and fences high enough to deter intrusion?

       B. Walls and fences obstruct surveillance of the yard and house?

       C. Walls and fences of sturdy construction?

       D. Gates of sturdy construction and have locks?

3. Locks

       A. All locks of high quality and sturdy construction?

       B. All locks (or key mechanisms) changed when moving in?

       C. All keys controlled and none left lying around?

       D. No door key hidden outside house?

       E. No house key left with shop when car repaired?

       F. No identification on keys or keychain?

       G. Locksmith well-known, reputable, and recommended?

       H. All locks locked at all times except when door, gate, etc., in use?

4. Landscaping

       A. Landscaping used to your security advantage?

       B. No high shrubbery close to house itself?

       C. No bushes or shrubbery close to house itself?

       D. High shrubbery or trees on perimeter of yard to shield house from observation?

5. Outdoor Lighting

       A. Outside lighting to illuminate yard?

       B. Lights for front door, porches, garage, etc.?

6. Have dog and use it effectively?

7. Have guards and use them effectively?

8. Have domestics and use them effectively?

9. Have internal safe haven with necessary emergency equipment and communications?

10. Alarm Systems

       A. Have alarms or warning devices which are good quality, effective, and appropriate to your needs?

       B. Use these alarm systems whenever possible?

11. You and your family practice good telephone security?

12. You and your family watch for surveillance of your home?
13. Everyone in your home understands who should have access and who should not?
14. Everyone in your home familiar with bomb detection and immediate actions in case one is suspected or found?
15. Take all precautions to leave home secure during your absence?
16. Vary your routines at and near home?
17. Practice good car-to-door security?
18. Family familiar with all your home security equipment and procedures?

OFFICE SECURITY

1. Office in safe location?
2. Office in modern, fireproof building?
3. Office in building with built-in security features and resident guard force?
4. Office above ground floor?
5. Guards effectively used?
6. Alarms and warning devices as appropriate?
7. Good telephone security procedures?
8. Staff familiar with bomb detection and response?
9. Access to office effectively controlled?
10. Office has emergency plans for various threat contingencies and staff is familiar with them?
11. Staff alert to surveillance of office?
12. Staff security officer treated as team member and suggestions followed?
13. Local employees fully checked before hiring?
14. Office maintains close and cordial relations with local authorities?
15. All staff members kept abreast of current threat situation?
16. Company and staff maintain as low a profile as possible?

CAR SECURITY AND DEFENSIVE DRIVING

1. Drive a car which provides a low profile in your area?
2. Equip your car with necessary security options?
3. Park your car in safe areas?
4. Practice good to-and-from car security?
5. Check your car for signs of tampering, bombs, and "breaking-in" before entry?
6. Know your car well, and familiar with handling characteristics and security systems?
7. Know your local area well?
8. Plan your routes?
9. Vary your routes, times, and routines?
10. Watch for surveillance?
11. Drive defensively?
12. Drive alertly?
13. Know how to recognize a vehicular attack situation?
14. Know the basic methods for escaping or countering an attack?
15. Familiar with post-attack actions?
16. Effectively use chauffeurs, bodyguards and chase cars in your defensive driving?

Checklist #7

BOTTOM LINE SECURITY

1. Have a gun and know how to use it?
2. Have a gun which is appropriate to your needs?
3. Have a gun which is legal and for which ammunition can be obtained?
4. Always handle your gun in a safe manner and keep it in a secure location?
5. Have non-lethal weapons which are appropriate to your situation?
6. Know how and when to use these weapons?
7. Have body armor which is effective and meets your needs?
8. Have body armor which is comfortable and can be worn clandestinely?
9. Have antiballistic briefcase?
10. Use your armor consistently?
11. Drive an armored car which suits your needs and requirements?
12. Armored car has necessary security systems and equipment?
13. Armoring is suitable to your area?
14. Know your armored car well, how it handles, and how all its systems operate?
15. Have guards appropriate to your needs?
16. Ensured that guards have passed background check?
17. Guards are honest, loyal, well trained, and understand your instructions?
18. Periodically check to see that guards are performing as required?
19. Have bodyguards that meet same basic requirements as

guards but have been professionally trained and perform in a like manner?

20. Know what civilian security services have to offer and know how to go about finding a good one?

TRIPS, TRAVEL, AND VACATIONS

1. Know the type and level of threat in the area you are visiting?
2. Have thoroughly planned your trip in regards to security?
3. Use the safest mode of travel?
4. Avoid high threat areas?
5. Stay at a safe and convenient location?
6. Ensure that your home is secure while you are away?
7. Keep all aspects of the trip confidential?
8. Vary your schedules and routines?
9. Maintain a low profile?
10. Make the best use of available security?

Checklist #9

SECURITY AND THE FAMILY

1. Understand the role your family plays in personal security?
2. Have included your family in your security planning?
3. Have instructed family members in their responsibilities regarding your personal security program?
4. Have taken special care to plan for the security of your children?
5. Have ensured good family communication and coordination regarding security?

Checklist #10

PREPARING FOR REALITIES

1. Have taken all necessary steps to prepare your family legally in the event of your kidnapping or death?
2. Have made sure that they will be provided for?
3. Have made sure they will know what actions to take and what actions not to take?
4. Know what actions your employer will take in this situation?
5. Have a close friend or associate outside of your family who will act according to your instructions and assist your family?
6. Know how to handle threats and extortion?
7. Understand the basic elements most often found in a violent attack in your area?
8. Know how these attacks are best handled?
9. Have made sure that your family knows what to do in the event of a violent attack?
10. Done all you can to prepare yourself and your family for a potential violent attack?
11. Understand how most kidnappings and hostage situations evolve?
12. Know what your immediate actions should be in the event you are involved in a kidnap or hostage situation?
13. Know how best to handle your captors?
14. Know what you should and should not do while being held captive?
15. Know what actions you should take after your release?